Classroom Matters

Weekly Leadership Lessons
And Inspiration
For Educators

Timothy M. Powers, Ed. D.

For additional information, contact the author at
timpowerswf@gmail.com

Visit the Author's Page at
www.amazon.com/author/timothympowers

Table of Contents

Introduction

If you are taking the time to read this introduction, then you are a part of the segment of people who do not just jump into the first chapter of a book because you understand that there is some reason for introductory material. You probably have a philosophy that if I am going to take the time to read the book, I want to get as much out of it as I possibly can. By following the suggestions in this introductory material, you will be well on your way to making a difference with students on an individual level.

Both educational leadership and growing as a leader are complex processes of seeing the big picture, evaluating the current situation and then, making decisions that will improve and move the organization forward. The organization for this specific context can be your classroom, your campus or your learning community, depending on where these leadership tools are implemented. In any of these situations, the important thing to remember is that it is in the *doing* that makes the difference. It is having the courage to try new things knowing that failure is a part of the process of success.

Perceptions of leadership vary as well, from the idea that leadership is just for campus administrators or central office staff to the idea that it is just for a select group.

However, the truth is that educational leadership is for everyone who touches the life of a student. This leadership development book may speak in terms of the classroom teacher, but anyone with access to students during the day can benefit from the leadership ideas and applications developed here.

These leadership lessons and principles focus on building an atmosphere and culture of success in the classroom, the campus and the learning community. These lessons are intended to cause the reader to deeply consider his/her beliefs about student learning and success and how each individual educator can significantly influence learning at the individual student level. These leadership tools are not intended to be a one-and-done process. It takes time and creating a culture of success is something that is sustainable with teachers and administrators who are willing to become courageous leaders for students and the educational process.

This book is intended for all levels of educators from the classroom teacher to the district superintendent. It is developed in a way for the individual to progress through the lessons on a weekly basis, providing time for the reader to pause, reflect, implement, and reflect again on the outcomes of the leadership development activities. This can be done individually or as a group book study. The outcome of growth is left up to you, the reader, as to the benefit that reading this book has on you and most importantly, your students, because that is the reason for this leadership development book and why you are reading it.

If you are like me, most educators do not have a large amount of time to dedicate to personal growth and improvement. The *Classroom Matters* lessons are purposely written to be brief and concise bite-sized nuggets of information because the intent is not just that you *know* something about the subject but that you *do* something with what you know. Too many of us have what I refer to as a Bible study mentality regarding leadership development. We are eager to know all about how to grow, but taking that information and *witnessing* or *doing* something with it can be a scary proposition. Most potential educational leaders have some leadership knowledge, but many are not willing to act on it because they are afraid of failure. We must overcome that fear of trying.

Many of the lessons are closely tied together and are specifically written to work together as well as emphasize very similar concepts. If you choose to read and attempt to apply these lessons as they are intended, your personal repertoire of leadership beliefs, skills, and mindsets will be enlarged and reinforced. Practicing skills is fundamental to improving yourself as a teacher and as a leader. Both are necessary for our educational systems to thrive and be productive. This is especially true if you want to shape and influence your classroom and campus culture to emphasize student academic achievement.

The suggested reading format will provide you with the best opportunity for leadership growth. First, read the lesson. If you are studying this with a group, then take a moment to discuss the lesson with them. If you are studying this book by yourself, then take a few minutes to reflect on the information. This is where most people miss a valuable part of the process. The act of reflecting helps the reader to begin to imbed the information in a personal way. It will allow the reader to make the leadership actions more meaningful. Equally important to reflecting is to understand that how you internalize this information may not be the same as your neighbor and that is okay. Next, follow the applications for the week; finally, record your responses to your application. Be sure to include both the good and the bad. Sometimes, the negative results can become more beneficial for you in the future than just the positive outcomes. Be sure to take this a week at a time. This is important. This leadership development book is intended for implementation and the building of leadership skills over time, to give you the time to use the material and to reflect on it as you develop your repertoire of leadership knowledge and tools.

The specific leadership application information is established in five areas. You will be given the leadership tool, encouraged to reflect, to apply, and to respond; then you will be given a deeper explanation of the leadership skillset. The *leadership tool* is the initial explanation of the specific principle of leadership. In the *leadership reflection,* you will be asked some questions to open your cognitive process of thinking about the leadership tool. In the *leadership application,* you will be encouraged to *do* something with that leadership principle. This is a part of leadership development that is important because in the doing, you are literally creating the myelin effect of the learning process, and the more you *do* it, the stronger those leadership skills become. By taking the time to write down your *leadership results*, you are confirming your work as an educational leader. You are reinforcing those leadership principles. Finally, the *leadership skillset* helps you to reinforce the four previous steps of leadership development and will help lock in the principle. Just remember that if you are serious about growing as an educational leader, these principles become alive and well the more that you do them.

This book challenges you to take risks, to be willing to get back up if you fail and try again. Shake the dust off your clothes when you get up, hold your head up and try again. You will find that just maybe the next time it works for you, and in it working for you, you are helping students to become academically successful. YOU made a difference in the life of a student just because you refused to accept failure as final. Congratulations on being willing to take risks for the sake of improving student achievement.

I have included a scripture for each week's lesson. I cannot imagine being an educator without the support and encouragement of the Lord. So many scriptures in the Bible serve as guidance and support as educators seek to make a difference in the lives of our young people. I pray the scripture references serve as a source of encouragement for you and help you in your daily walk with Him.

Lesson 1: Keep Hope Alive

No one ever thought it could be done, but when Roger Bannister ran the "miracle mile" in 1954, the world was stunned. He had broken through a barrier that was once thought unbreakable. He had run a mile in less than four minutes. Roger Bannister never gave up hope that one day he would achieve what others thought was impossible. He *kept hope alive*. Although he had to run the race, he did not go it alone. In the race he had runners pacing him and encouraging him all along the way to make sure he did not fall off the pace. It was not until the last two hundred yards that he sprinted ahead and finished in front.

This milestone was never accomplished in recorded history prior to Roger Bannister, and yet, less than two months later, another person ran the mile in less than four minutes. How could something that seemed so unreachable become such an achievable goal? The answer lies in *hope*. This *hope* was kept alive in the hearts of those who believed that success was possible.

This same *hope* lies within every child who enters our classrooms. It is an inherent trait in all of us. However, as easily as a limb or extremity can be removed from the body, this *hope* can be ripped from the hearts and the minds of our students. Stiggins[1] (2003) states, "Do not deprive of hope" in helping all students to achieve academic success.

The teachers in the classroom are a daily reminder that we keep this *hope* alive in our students. It is a source of renewal to observe teachers, paraprofessionals and other staff refusing to allow students to quit or fail when an academic goal is not reached, even when students become frustrated because of the instructional challenges that face them. It is a constant source of encouragement to observe teachers who refuse to allow failure to be final and who recognize that success lies just around the corner in a different instructional approach, a different learning style or just more time to absorb the content.

The concept of *hope* is a source of encouragement for our students. So many of our students' struggles are aligned with many forms of learning disabilities, and many of those disabilities remain undiagnosed. Yet, as educators our responsibility is to continue to encourage academic growth for all our students as we meet those learning challenges head-on.

Can we achieve the high standards of academic success we have established for ALL of our students? Roger Bannister did not go it alone. He succeeded with the help of others. We will too. In addition, as we begin to achieve some measure of academic success, it will begin to become commonplace. How will we get there? We will get there with the help of each other and by *keeping hope alive* in our students and ourselves.

Leadership Application

LEADERSHIP TOOL: *Keep hope alive in ALL of your students!* We are educators. We are encouragers for all students, especially in times of academic struggle. Our contracts do not state anywhere that we can stop teaching or give up on a child, even when he/she appears to not want to learn. No, you may not be successful with each student, but do not be the one to extinguish the hope that is embedded in the heart of each of those students.

LEADERSHIP REFLECTION: Think about the students you have or will be receiving. Using the lesson information, make a mental note of what attitudes and behaviors you must improve upon to keep hope alive. Once you have done that, write yourself a "personal commitment" statement (short statement of a paragraph or less) and place that statement in your room or office where it is visible for you to review on a regular basis, especially when you are frustrated and feel the urge to just give up on a student.

LEADERSHIP APPLICATION: Take the time to review your students' folders and see if you can identify some actions and strategies that would help you spark student interest and mastery of learning material for the students.

Then, select one student who is being challenged in academic mastery and try just one strategy that might help that student achieve academic success in an area in which he/she is struggling. One idea to help unlock the student's potential is to identify the student's area of interest(s) and try to create an instructional strategy that addresses one of the student's academic weaknesses. Go ahead and try it!

LEADERSHIP RESULTS: This is an important part of growing as an educator and as an instructional leader. Take a moment to enter your thoughts in the journal space (as suggested in the introduction) and take a few minutes to reflect on this week's application. Was the application successful? What were some indicators of success? What were the indicators of failure (this is important)? What can you do differently to improve on this particular leadership tool?

RESPONSE:

_____

_____

_____

_____

_____

LEADERSHIP SKILL SET: You are developing the skillset of being an encourager. You are keeping hope alive. To develop this skill, make a note to challenge yourself on a regular basis and to continue to identify students who need to have their learning potential unlocked. Remember not to be too hard on yourself when the results may not be exactly what you had envisioned. Students need to know for certain that you believe in them, even in the most challenging times. Remember, your skill set here is to keep hope alive!

I pray that the eyes of your heart may be enlightened in order
that you may know the hope to which He has called you,
the riches of His glorious inheritance in His holy people.
Ephesians 1:18 NKJV

Lesson 2: Beginning with the End in Mind

Operation Overlord, better known as D-Day has been recorded in history as one of the greatest invasions ever orchestrated. This was the day that the combined Allied Forces landed on the beaches of Normandy and began their assault and eventual victory over the regime of Adolf Hitler. The successful invasion and ultimate victory over Hitler and his forces did not begin on the battlegrounds of Normandy. The success of the outcome began in the meticulous planning and decision-making with the ultimate objective in mind. Many accounts record no less than six months of detailed, focused planning which served as an example of *beginning with the end in mind* for the Allied Forces.

Poverty and ignorance continue to be roadblocks to students on becoming productive, responsible, contributing members of a prosperous society. The classroom is our battleground and our beachhead for the educational lives of our students and society. We must also *begin with the end in mind* if we are to take a stand against poverty and ignorance in our classrooms and our community. We must meticulously plan to eradicate this poverty and ignorance.

What is essential for our intended outcome to be reached? We must all be on the same page as to what our goal is for our students. In its simplest form, our goal is to ensure that every student achieves academic success by whatever standards are placed before us at the local, state and at the national level. When *beginning with the end in mind*, we understand what that means as we prepare to meet those standards with ALL students.

Beginning with the end in mind involves great planning, and planning involves intensive collaboration. Collaboration involves sharing the best ideas and practices among teachers and staff including what works and what is a work in progress. Communication of every detail of the learning process with others results in greater success for students.

Deep practice, with students focusing on readiness skills, is an additional requirement for *beginning with the end in mind*. Daniel Coyle[2] (2009) states that "deep practice is built on a paradox: struggling in certain targeted ways, operating at the edges of your ability where you make mistakes…makes you smarter." Put another way, we need to teach our students that struggle and failure are a part of success. This process allows us to ultimately reach our intended goal: for every student to achieve those academic success standards identified at the local, state, and national levels.

Beginning with the end in mind will always include *quality teaching*. This has been and always will be a cornerstone of student success. Teachers who are prepared and who have a laser-like focus on helping every student achieve academic success understand the importance of their role. Prepared teachers have studied the material extensively, understand the concepts to be taught and have communicated the instructional objectives to the students, so the students know what the instructional goals and expectations are for them.

We have an instructional beachhead to attack, and we must go in with the confidence that we possess the people and the resources to help our students achieve academic mastery. Classroom teachers are the first line of attack on ignorance, and we will be successful if we are preparing, *beginning with the end in mind.*

Leadership Application

LEADERSHIP TOOL: *Be prepared by knowing what your students must master to be academically successful! Begin with the end in mind.* Take the time to review your local, state and national standards. If time does not permit, then identify your state expectations. To know those standards means to understand them and to be able to teach them as they would be tested for mastery with the students.

LEADERSHIP REFLECTION: If you have ever looked at the requirements of state objectives, you have become overwhelmed with the amount of material required for students to learn. Learning and mastering the material to be taught should not be done alone. Think about whom you know that you can collaborate, communicate and plan with in trying to identify and understand the critical learning objectives for your students. What do you think deep practice means? Take a moment to develop a mental concept of that idea and paraphrase your concept of deep learning in your journal.

LEADERSHIP APPLICATION: Does your campus participate in collaborating through professional learning communities or something similar where you can talk with other teachers who are teaching your grade or subject level? Use that professional learning community to take one subject and ask your colleagues what they feel are the most important critical learning objectives for that area. Educators need to have embedded many of those critical learning attributes in their memory to be able to *begin with the end in mind.*

LEADERSHIP RESULTS: This is an important part of growing as an educator and as an instructional leader. Take a moment to enter your thoughts in the journal space (as suggested in the introduction) and take a few minutes to reflect on this week's application. Was the application successful? What were some indicators of success? What were the indicators of failure (this is important)? What can

you do differently to improve on this particular leadership tool?

RESPONSE:

_____

_____

_____

_____

_____

LEADERSHIP SKILL SET: To develop this skill, always *begin with the end in mind*, so that your goal as an educator is to prepare your students to achieve success on those standards that have been established at the local, state and national levels with an emphasis on the state standards. It is always more beneficial to utilize your professional learning communities to keep yourself and others focused on understanding what those objectives for students are and how the students will demonstrate mastery. Encourage your team to keep your "end in mind" goals on the agenda for most, if not all meetings. By doing this, you are beginning to create a culture that is focused on student academic success.

But you, be strong and do not let your hands be weak,
for your work shall be rewarded!
2 Chronicles 17:7 NKJV

Lesson 3: Building Relationships - A Building Block for Academic Success

I never cease to be amazed whenever I am privy to conversations about how one person was positively influenced by another. The amazement is not that the person was influenced but that he or she often names a teacher who was instrumental in guiding him or her toward a successful path in life. The other evening I was watching one of the late night television shows, and the host was asking a movie celebrity about who influenced her. After some discussion about her problems in school, she named a particular teacher who made a significant impact on her success.

It was what the celebrity shared that caught my attention though. She said, "This teacher had been quietly observing me and pulled me aside and told me that I was not living up to my potential and that I could do much better. She believed in me, and I believed her." I did not really pay attention as to who the celebrity was or how well the person was doing now, but it did stick with me that some of the measure of success she was experiencing, she attributed to a teacher.

This was another reminder to me of how important and influential we are in the lives of the students we see and come into contact with on a daily basis. It is especially important for us to remember the idea of *building relationships*. In numerous articles, research states that one major factor in closing the achievement gap for low-performing students, especially those who are identified as economically disadvantaged, is *building* healthy *relationships*.

I recently re-read an updated version of Ruby Payne's book on children in poverty, and one of the major themes of the book was *building relationships*. She was quick to add that it does not cure all children, but it does make a difference. Payne[3] (2006) stated that educators can *build* healthy *relationships* by utilizing support systems, by having a sincere concern for the student through caring, by promoting student achievement, by being a role model and by insisting upon successful behaviors for school.

The successful teachers that I observe on a weekly basis on campuses and in learning communities are doing just what Dr. Ruby Payne suggests. Do your colleagues and staff take the time to *build relationships*? You can begin building relationships today with plenty of opportunities to touch lives forever. Thank you for taking the time to invest in your students to *build relationships* that will help students to achieve academic success. Moreover, just think, YOU are the catalyst for that success!

Leadership Application

LEADERSHIP TOOL: *The leadership tool that you are trying to develop here is the skill for developing healthy relationships. Keep in mind that every student with whom you come into contact should have the opportunity to be touched and developed through a relational contact.* There will be degrees of relationship building with the amount of time that you are able to spend with the students. The exciting part is that you may never know what encounter will have that lasting impact on an individual.

LEADERSHIP REFLECTION: Think about the many opportunities that you have to interact with students. Are there times when you avoid relationship building moments because the structure of the day discourages this? When you are talking to small groups or individual students, do you give them your full attention? Do you take the time to delve into their world of concerns to discern if there is an opportunity for you to demonstrate your interest in them? Think about what you can do to change your mindset regarding building relationships.

LEADERSHIP APPLICATION: Depending on the time of year, your students probably already have a good handle on who you are and what classroom mannerisms you possess. If you are like most classroom teachers, you are multi-tasking just to be able to get the must-do job expectations completed.

I would challenge you to give your full attention to some designated students in your day this week. Be intentional in your actions. Stop what you are doing, focus directly on the student or group and give them the full focus of your attention. Confirm it by repeating the conversation back to the individual or group so they know you were listening intently. If the discussion calls for a solution, offer some ideas and encourage them to complete the task. Also, throw in a genuine compliment for their expected efforts and let them know that you will follow-up on their task. This is where the trench work begins and the relationships are built and cultivated. The moment that you actually follow-up and listen with the same intensity, you will have that student's or group's respect. That respect translates into academic productivity at times.

LEADERSHIP RESULTS: This is an important part of growing as an educator and as an instructional leader. Take a moment to enter your thoughts in the journal space (as suggested in the introduction) and take a few minutes to reflect on this week's application. Was the application successful? What were some indicators of success? What were the indicators of failure (this is important)? What can you do differently to improve on this particular leadership tool?

RESPONSE:

_____

_____

_____

_____

_____

LEADERSHIP SKILL SET: To develop this skill, you must be intentional about being focused on conversations and listen more than you speak. Remember that to build relationships you will need time and a conscientious effort on your part to pay attention and to give good sound advice. Sometimes, the advice is less important than the student(s) knowing that you are an active listener. This skill takes more than a week worth of practice, but it is a starting point. As you begin to see the fruition of your investment of time through relationship building, then you can begin to hone in on specific students that could benefit greatly from your investment.

Therefore comfort each other and edify one another, just as you also are doing.
I Thessalonians 5:11 NKJV

Lesson 4: Quality Teaching - Another Building Block for Academic Success

Anyone connected to sports, and certainly those who are students of basketball, would probably connect the name "Wizard of Westwood" quite easily with John Wooden. Wooden garnered ten national basketball championships in a twelve-year period while coaching at UCLA. Even though he retired from coaching four decades ago, he is still considered by most sports analysts as one of the greatest basketball coaches. However, he always referred to himself as a teacher rather than a coach. The basketball court was his classroom. He taught his "students" more about life and how to be successful in life than he did about the game of basketball. It was his *quality teaching* that made him a great coach.

Quality teaching is another one of the four building blocks for student academic success. The type of *quality teaching* I am referring to is an active, engaged, participatory type of teaching that transforms the classroom into a laboratory for life's lessons. It is teaching in anticipation and with the understanding that the unexpected will come with every lesson every day, realizing that through our repertoire of quality teaching tools; we will help every child achieve academic success by engaging them in authentic learning.

The research is replete with studies that point to *quality teaching* as the number one factor in improving student academic success. In a Gallup Poll released in the September 2010 issue of Phi Delta Kappan (http://www.kappanmagazine.org/content/92/1/9.full.pdf+html), Americans said the number one priority in education should be improving the quality of teachers. It is certainly one of the major factors to closing the achievement gap that exists among our highest and lowest performing student populations. Thernstrom and Thernstrom[4] (2004) state *quality teaching* as the key to excellent schools achieving academic success.

What are those characteristics of *quality teaching* that motivate students to achieve our academic goals we have established for them? It begins with our individual teacher behaviors about student learning that shape attitudes, which in turn, transform a campus into a culture of academic success. We move from an emphasis on teaching in the classroom to a focus on student learning. It is a shift from traditional grading to assessment *FOR* learning. It is an understanding that learning takes place in a variety of activities and venues because we recognize our students learn differently and at different rates. It is teachers finding a way when the first or second try at learning does not work.

I see it. I see it every day I go into the classrooms. No, I do not see it in every classroom, but the more I visit classes, the more I see the change in behavior, in attitude and a reshaping of the culture of academic success. I see teachers who have prepared for success before the first student steps into the classroom. I see you, the teacher, at work modeling quality teaching, and our students are the benefactors.

Leadership Application

LEADERSHIP TOOL: *This leadership tool is quality teaching. It is preparing yourself to give your students your utmost and an opportunity of being successful on the standards that have been set by you, your campus, your learning community and the state.* This requires a certain amount of organizational skills and preparation on your part. Do not misinterpret quality teaching with a quality teacher. A quality teacher is one with high teaching credentials. Quality teaching is one who has invested the blood, sweat and tears into preparation, making sure the right information and instructional tools have been selected for the task. It means being prepared for the unexpected.

LEADERSHIP REFLECTION: Do you spend time prior to your students entering your classroom making sure that you have aligned your teaching plans to present information that the students are expected to learn? Have you invested in multiple forms of presentations to engage your students in the learning process? Do your lessons achieve the depth and complexity needed for your students to master to the degree they will be assessed? Is there a professional set of expectations with you and among your colleagues that preparation is a key ingredient to quality teaching?

LEADERSHIP APPLICATION: Evaluate your preparation time for presenting the week's lessons. Spend some time to make sure the critical attributes you are teaching for the week are indeed standards that will be assessed or are supporting standards that are necessary for student academic success. Review the activities you have planned. Make sure that the activities you have selected reinforce the learning material and that they are activities that will engage the students in the learning process. This may take a little more time on your part, but the investment you make up front will pay dividends on the other side of the lesson presentation.

LEADERSHIP RESULTS: This is an important part of growing as an educator and as an instructional leader. Take a moment to enter your thoughts in the journal space (as suggested in the introduction) and take a few minutes to reflect on this week's application. Was the application successful? What were some indicators of success? What were the indicators of failure (this is important)? What can you do differently to improve on this particular leadership tool?

RESPONSE:

_____

_____

_____

_____

_____

LEADERSHIP SKILL SET: You are always becoming a quality teacher. It is an evolving process because your students are constantly changing as well as the research and technology which serve our students. As with any business or work of art achieving quality takes time, determination and resolve. Be patient with yourself, but also demand more of yourself during the process. This stretch will allow you to surprise yourself during your growth periods in becoming a quality teacher. Your direct input into becoming a quality teacher will translate into improved academic success and a culture that focuses on higher expectations for all students.

**...in all things showing yourself *to be* a
pattern of good works;
in doctrine *showing* integrity, reverence, incorruptibility,
sound speech that cannot be condemned,
one who is an opponent may be ashamed,
having nothing evil to say of you.
Titus 2:7-8 NKJV**

Lesson 5: High Expectations - A Third Building Block for Academic Success

The Soviet Union had beaten the United States to space by launching the Sputnik in 1957, signifying the beginning of the space age. This single event shocked the public and put the US back on its heels. It also ignited NASA's determination in the 1960s to be the first nation to place a man on the face of the moon and return him safely within the decade. Although this task was seen as virtually impossible in the early sixties, the *high expectations* set by our nation's president in 1961 were the first steps in attaining this goal. In addition, many of the components necessary to achieve this goal had not even been invented when this idea of placing a man on the moon was first conceived. Yet because of these *high expectations*, the US never gave up on meeting its goal, which it accomplished on July 20, 1969.

That same spirit and determination of establishing *high expectations* for our students must continue with the belief that all children can achieve academic success at or above grade level. *High expectations*, along with the appropriate support and resources, will provide the necessary scaffolding for our students to achieve these academic standards. Reeves[5] (2006) stated that adults make a difference in student achievement, and adults are also helpless bystanders in student learning. In other words, we make a difference when we set *high expectations* and then do something to help our students achieve their goals.

We are competing against ignorance, plain and simple. Establishing *high expectations* for all students makes it possible for more students to move out of ignorance and become successful contributors to our society. The support and resources we give as educators, as well as modeling the idea of life-long learning, provide the stair steps for students to step out of ignorance and into academic success. The necessary support and resources go hand-in-hand with high expectation. Not having the appropriate support and resources is like telling a high jumper he/she can clear a certain height without telling him/her how to do it. Teacher in-service and training help teachers with giving them the information and additional instructional ideas to provide students with the scaffolding they need to be successful as they raise their level of expectation for students.

Therefore, as educators, we arm ourselves with support for students by utilizing proven research-based methods to help our students achieve academically. While we are learning and constantly finding better ways to help our students, we do hold them accountable for actually learning the material, not for just being present during the lesson. We set *high expectations* for students and do not let them "off the hook" by accepting failure. We require learning through a teaching and re-teaching process and reassessing when the learning of the material is not initially demonstrated. These *high expectations* help students overcome the learning challenges that seem almost impossible at the beginning; but like the race to the moon, teachers in our classrooms make the impossible possible each and every day.

Leadership Application

LEADERSHIP TOOL: *This leadership tool is that of developing a mindset that setting high expectations will yield instructional academic returns. This high expectation tool must be accompanied with your ability to produce the appropriate support and resources to scaffold the student learning and demonstration of the mastery skills.* Developing this tool may require you to step back and re-evaluate your personal philosophy of educating students. It also requires teachers to be lifelong learners, always seeking a better way to help our students.

LEADERSHIP REFLECTION: Do you truly believe that all students can learn at high rates of academic success? Do you catch yourself automatically limiting student's ability to achieve success because of his/hers initial failures or a previous teacher's comments? Do you base your students' ability to succeed on the support you are receiving from the students' home-life? Is your campus' culture for learning such that all students are expected to learning at a high rate of mastery?

LEADERSHIP APPLICATION: Seriously evaluate your personal perspective on student achievement and your expectations for student mastery. Once you have determined for yourself what you believe high expectations for your students are, make a plan to discuss with your students those expectations and make sure that you include with your plans that you will support their learning process with the support and resources they need. To complete this activity you will need to be direct about a specific learning activity. If you have been somewhat negligent in this area, your students may raise an eyebrow or two and test your resolve so make sure your support is genuine and meaningful. In doing so, you will begin to establish a safety net for student learning.

LEADERSHIP RESULTS: This is an important part of growing as an educator and as an instructional leader. Take a moment to enter your thoughts in the journal space (as suggested in the introduction) and take a few minutes to reflect on this week's application. Was the application successful? What were some indicators of success? What were the indicators of failure (this is important)? What can you do differently to improve on this particular leadership tool?

RESPONSE:

_____

_____

_____

_____

_____

LEADERSHIP SKILL SET: This is a great skillset to develop and it may take some time for your students to buy in to the fact that you genuinely do care about their learning and mastery of the material. You will need to read (part of life-long learning) about ways to support student learning. Find what research is telling us about learning and the brain research that is out there like the myelin effect. When you set those expectations high and truly "*expect*" performance to rise, then you will be amazed at the results. However, try not to act too surprised in front of the students!

As each one has received a gift, minister it to one another, as good stewards of the manifold grace of God.
I Peter 4:10 NKJV

Lesson 6: Time - The Final Building Block for Academic Success

Time is such an abstract concept to many people. For some, it is a momentary glance at the clock to determine when to be at the next meeting or function. For small children, it is merely a set of episodic events such as a *time* to eat, a *time* to play, a *time* to read or a *time* to go to bed. No matter how one views *time*, it is arguably one of the most important functions of each of our lives. Many of you reading this lesson at the moment probably have access to a wrist watch or a cell phone displaying the *time* or maybe even a clock on a desk or a wall that you have not glanced at for some *time*…until now.

The concept of *time* has major implications in education. For students in need of additional academic help and who are not afforded the *time* to fully understand a concept, the lack of *time* becomes a huge impediment to learning. However, a teacher who provides that extra *time* to help a student excel in the learning process could literally make the difference between the student mastering the information or continuing to fall further behind. The use of additional *time* in this way can become the equalizer for many students, placing more of them in the "mastered" category; however, when we don't provide this opportunity of additional *time* for students who need it to internalize the critical learning objectives, the gaps in their education become greater and the learning process for them is compounded by having to learn material connected to information they have not previously mastered.

Anyone who has taught in the classroom for even a minimal length of *time* understands that students do not learn at the same rate. Educators realize that instead of viewing *time* as a *constant*, it should become a *variable* and a resource to improve student achievement. DuFour[6] (2004) states that some students will require more *time* to learn and that schools need to develop strategies to provide students with that *time* during the school day. Here is where the professional learning communities provide a great opportunity for discussion to create a specific body of time for that purpose. This collaboration could mean the difference between success or failure for a significant number of students.

One can begin to see how the four major characteristics of academic success (building relationships, quality teaching, high expectations and providing additional *time* for students to learn) all begin to fit together to provide an ever increasing opportunity for students to achieve those academic standards. Students who need additional instructional or processing *time* to be successful in the classroom see teachers who provide this as caring and concerned individuals who refuse to give up on them. Students see these teachers as individuals who are willing to do whatever it takes to help them succeed.

Many learning communities are transforming from a culture of teaching to a culture of learning. There is a difference. If we are to continue our necessary progression to focus more on student learning and create a results oriented culture, we must recognize and embrace the different learning rates of our students and hold them responsible for the material, even when it takes more *time*. Making that one allowance as a teacher while keeping your expectations for learning the material will make all the difference.

Leadership Application

LEADERSHIP TOOL: *This leadership tool is learning how to allocate time. All educators must understand the importance of this particular variable as it relates to individual students and the variance of the learning process for each of them.* Teachers must expand their view of how time for instruction and non-instructional activities are used throughout the school day and be creative in finding ways for learners to obtain more time to learn the designated material. **LEADERSHIP REFLECTION**: Do you have all your students scheduled on the same pace for learning? Have you ever stopped to evaluate the causes of student failure might be that the student needs more time to complete the assignment? Do you provide opportunities for students to redo or rework the assignment because it does not meet your expectation for mastery? Have you considered making time a variable in the learning process rather than the constant? Are you more concerned about the student's grade than if he/she learned the material?

LEADERSHIP APPLICATION: Review your current practices related to student mastery. Do you require all students to turn in work at the same time? Is time used as a measure of student mastery? Have you ever considered placing more emphasis on <u>what</u> the student knows rather than <u>when</u> the student masters it? Is there a way that you could provide additional time for learning during the school day for your students who need more time to master the material?

LEADERSHIP RESULTS: This is an important part of growing as an educator and as an instructional leader. Take a moment to enter your thoughts in the journal space (as suggested in the introduction) and take a few minutes to reflect on this week's application. Was the application successful? What were some indicators of success? What were the indicators of failure (this is important)? What can you do differently to improve on this particular leadership tool?

RESPONSE:

_____

_____

_____

_____

_____

LEADERSHIP SKILL SET: Your skillset here is to understand the value of providing more time for your students to master the material. Providing more time does not mean you are lowering your expectations for learning. In fact, it means just the opposite. It means you are willing to find different ways for students to learn what you have deemed important. Understand that not all students learn at the same rate. Some notice it faster than others do. That does not make them smarter, just faster. Learning should not be a race; it should be a process set on a continuum of critical learning objectives that all students must be held accountable for learning.

**See then that you walk circumspectly,
not as fools but as wise,
redeeming the time, because the days are evil.
Therefore do not be unwise,
but understand what the will of the Lord _is_.
Ephesians 5:15-17 NKJV**

Lesson 7: Spheres of Influence

Our planet is unique; to date it is the only planet that we are aware of which is capable of sustaining life as we know it. Its uniqueness is a direct result of the *sphere of influence* that the sun, moon and orbit in our solar system have on it. Think about it; our planet is tilted at approximately 23.4 degrees, and this, along with its rotation around the sun, provides us with our seasonal changes. We are also situated far enough away from the sun not to be incinerated by its extreme heat, yet we are close enough to provide the right amount of warmth to sustain life. This *sphere of influence* is also extended to our moon, which is part of the phenomenon of low and high tides in our oceans' shores. These appropriate *spheres of influence* are one of the reasons that allow us to inhabit this place called earth.

Spheres of influence also exist within our learning organization through a psychological phenomenon in the daily interactions of teachers and students in the classroom. Every person in our learning organization has a certain amount of influence on every other person. I am reminded of the quote by Sir Alfred Lord Tennyson[7] (1883) in his poem, "Ulysses," when he said, "I am a part of all that I have met." The truth of this statement resounds with comparable influence in the classroom. The students that enter our classrooms become an opportunity for us to "influence" them toward academic success. What we say, what we do and how we react are monitored and registered even by our most challenging students, and they catalogue those influences in their life experiences with each student making an individual determination as to his/her self-worth. They evaluate our expectations for their success by the influences we project upon them as our students. Let us be reminded of the cornerstones of successful education as we realize that we are one of the major *spheres of influence* in the lives of our students.

We must utilize this knowledge of being a *sphere of influence* by building healthy relationships with our students, providing quality teaching and learning experiences that tie new knowledge to old learning, setting high expectations while providing the appropriate support and resources to allow students to achieve academic success and provide the time that each student needs to realize that success. This *sphere of influence* can impact each of these areas.

Our learning culture must understand the importance that we serve as *spheres of influence* and must capitalize on the attributes listed above in a way that will move our students forward in the learning continuum. Accept the challenge to be one of the *spheres of influence* for your students in our learning culture and to focus on quality teaching, building relationships, establishing high expectations and providing the time for our students to achieve academic success.

We are not allowed to decide if we are to be *spheres of influence*. The moment we accepted the opportunity to serve in any part of the educational system that responsibility became ours as a treasured gift. Become that *sphere of influence* for your classroom that you would want someone else to be for your own child. Make such a difference with all of your students that when they are leaving your classroom for the last time, you will be able to whisper to yourself, "I am a part of all that I have met" and know that your *sphere of influence* has made a positive difference in the lives of your students.

Leadership Application

LEADERSHIP TOOL: *You are building the leadership tool of understanding your role using your sphere of influence. You will need to understand that there is an opportunity on your part to use this tool as an instrument for improving academic performance as well as shaping the academic culture of your classroom.* There is a real physiological phenomenon related to physical proximity called sphere of influence. This tool carries this beyond just the physical proximity to influence the students' mental processes and capacities related to mastering the identified academic standards.

LEADERSHIP REFLECTION: Have you ever conscientiously thought of how you have the ability to influence the attitudes and atmosphere of your students' classroom? Do you ever use your physical proximity to control classroom behavior and order? Have you taken this same principle to the next level and considered your mental proximity (the classroom) and how you can establish the culture of high expectations and an attitude of success? How does your classroom sphere of influence compare with other classrooms around you? Are you using this as an opportunity to positively shape the academic culture of your classroom?

LEADERSHIP APPLICATION: Identify those standards under the four cornerstones or building blocks of academic success (quality teaching, high expectations, building relationships and providing time to master the material) that would allow you to begin using your sphere of influence to create a culture of learning and success. If other teachers or staff members are reading this book with you, compare notes to see if you can add to your list or help others clarify theirs.

LEADERSHIP RESULTS: This is an important part of growing as an educator and as an instructional leader. Take a moment to enter your thoughts in the journal space (as suggested in the introduction) and take a few minutes to

reflect on this week's application. Was the application successful? What were some indicators of success? What were the indicators of failure (this is important)? What can you do differently to improve on this particular leadership tool?

RESPONSE:

_____

_____

_____

_____

_____

LEADERSHIP SKILL SET: You are developing the ability to capitalize on using your sphere of influence to affect student learning in a positive and successful manner. It is a tool that can become extremely useful as well as powerful once you have learned to properly control each situation that would allow you to influence your students' learning processes. This is a teaching tool and not a manipulation tool that becomes stronger and more effective as you "grow" with your students throughout the year, and you are able to develop the four building blocks for academic success. When used properly and for the right reasons, your students will prosper and hold you in high regard, as well as creating that desired atmosphere for productive learning to occur.

**Let your light so shine before men,
that they may see your good works
and glorify your Father in heaven.
Matthew 5:17 NKJV**

Lesson 8: A Piece of the Puzzle

I used to love putting puzzles together when I was growing up and I still do. One of our Christmas rituals, while our children were still living at home, was to complete one of those 1,000 plus piece puzzles. Well, you can imagine with four people working on the puzzle at different times, we were always looking for the last couple of pieces and were determined to find them on the floor. It got to where at least one or more members of the family would attempt to keep a piece back so she/he could be the one to complete the puzzle. It just never seemed complete without every piece of the puzzle being placed together properly. What a sense of accomplishment we felt when we were done!

Our learning organization can be viewed as one giant instructional puzzle, and each employee is a *piece of the puzzle*. Better yet, we represent the edges of this huge puzzle we call education. We all fit together seamlessly to form the frame of this wonderful educational process, and it is our responsibility to turn over each *piece of the puzzle*, better known as students, and help place them where they will be most successful. As the edge of the puzzle, we help to create a framework that will allow us to place every student accordingly.

Every student - every *piece of the puzzle* - counts. Each person who is employed by your learning organization is responsible for your students' successes. What will each of us do? What will we expect our students to do so that we can make sure they are successfully placed on this canvas of learning continuum that we call education?

Will we allow some of them to fall off the table and not look for them? Will we turn them back over so we cannot see their "faces" and be less bothered because we cannot successfully place them? Will we hand the "piece" off to someone else because it is too difficult for us to find the place of success?

What is required is leadership and leadership courage in all of us to resolve to make this learning process the best possible year for our students to achieve academic success. It is being able to instill a sense of intrinsic motivation within our students that creates a drive, which eventually leads to the academic success we want all our students to achieve. Through building proper relationships with our students, we can create in them what Pink[8] (2009) refers to as "Type I" behavior, a way of thinking that occurs within students that helps them understand that they can capitalize on their innate need to direct their own lives. Each person in your organization can touch the life of a student in such a way that the student begins to feel empowered and in control of his/her own learning process. As it is now, many students believe they are trapped within a particular course of learning where there is no hope of escape. The beauty of education is that educators can show them a better way, a more prosperous path using academic success as the vehicle for prosperity.

When we are engaged in putting a puzzle together and we come across a piece of the puzzle that we cannot fit, we place it down and return to it as the picture comes into focus. We do not throw the piece away because it did not fit the first time we tried it. I would challenge you to be steadfast in your determination to view each of your students as a piece of the puzzle that we call education and that each of your students will become a part of the success of education rather than become a discarded piece of an incomplete puzzle. You be that catalyst for student success!

Leadership Application

LEADERSHIP TOOL: *Consider each student in your classroom as a significant piece of your personal educational puzzle.* Just like beginning with a thousand pieces, it is challenging to see how it will all come together. Your objective is to make sure each piece, each student is successfully placed in the education system. Your objective is to provide the spark within them to ignite them that will help them understand intrinsic motivational learning is the key to academic success.

LEADERSHIP REFLECTION: Our students are coming to us from complex homes and family settings. Think what you can do to gain more knowledge and understanding of a few of the more challenging students that are in your classes. Have you ever just let a student "fall off the table" and not try to recover the student? What do you think it means to have leadership courage in this situation? Are you willing to make a difference in this area? What are some ways to spark that intrinsic motivation within our students? How can we capitalize in that Type 1 behavior that will help students to capitalize on their need to direct their own lives?

LEADERSHIP APPLICATION: You have one or more students who could easily fall off the table of education. Look more closely at their student files to get a better idea of their past educational challenges. Do not just look at their test scores. Dig a little deeper and talk to prior teachers and teacher aides to see if you can find a pattern of student issues and concerns. See if you can identify one thing that you can do differently in the life of one or more students. Are you willing to bring that student in to be a part of the puzzle?

LEADERSHIP RESULTS: This is an important part of growing as an educator and as an instructional leader. Take a moment to enter your thoughts in the journal space (as suggested in the introduction) and take a few minutes to reflect on this week's application. Was the application successful? What were some indicators of success? What were the indicators of failure (this is important)? What can you do differently to improve on this particular leadership tool?

RESPONSE:

_____

_____

_____

_____

_____

LEADERSHIP SKILL SET: To develop this skill, remember that every student is a *piece of the puzzle* and every student counts. Your goal is making sure all of the students will be successfully placed and that your puzzle will be complete. Your students will challenge YOU to complete the puzzle by hiding their "issues" because like all of us, they do not like to admit to not being able to meet the rigorous academic standards that have been established. Your challenge is to develop this skill set and help them fit in and begin to take responsibility of their learning goals!

**All Scripture *is* given by inspiration of God,
and *is* profitable for doctrine,
for reproof, for correction, for instruction in
righteousness,**

that the man of God may be complete, thoroughly equipped for every good work.

2 Timothy 3:16-17 NKJV

Lesson 9: The Energizing Educator

I always get a kick out of watching the creativity that is put into the "Energizer Bunny" battery commercials and the company's attempt to convince you of the superiority and longevity of their battery. The fact of the matter is that even those batteries eventually run down and have no energy left to help you power the flashlight or any other instrument that needs energy to operate.

In a similar sense, we operate off a need for physical, emotional, psychological and spiritual energy to be able to function successfully during the day. To be an *energizing educator*, we need to be replenished and recharged in all of these areas on a regular basis. The culture of a successful learning organization requires us to be mindful of this process so that we can continue to be successful in helping all of our students achieve academic success. To ignore signs of depletion in these areas is a signal that negative outcomes are just around the corner. Those negative outcomes may manifest themselves in areas such as declining personal health, lack of concern for student achievement or safety and depression.

An *energizing educator* is one who is capable of sharing his/her energy with those around him/her through the many processes and opportunities we have to demonstrate leadership. Although there are four frames of cognition (structural, political, symbolic and human resource) that lend themselves to improving the success of a learning organization, one in particular serves as a catalyst for the *energizing educator* who is willing to lead those around them by example. This frame of cognition is referred to by Bolman and Deal[9] (1997) as the "Symbolic Frame". This frame serves as the energy creator for the *energizing educator* who understands the power of emotional and psychological fission and who realizes that when this energy is shared through positive professional learning communities and by subject and grade-level meetings, the energy is split and multiplied. Others catch the energy and benefit from it. You in turn, benefit from their re-energizing as well. Sharing with each other through the many different forms of staff development is a source of renewal for educators. Educators are able to recharge their systems when this staff development is presented in a way to provide educators with resources and support.

The culture of a learning organization thrives on this type of educational fission demonstrated in both a sharing with and supporting of others in focusing on student academic success. An *energizing educator* shares and builds energy with other staff members by understanding, accepting and promoting the mission, vision, values and core commitments of the organization. This energy is expanded exponentially when these beliefs are demonstrated in improving measurable student success. This becomes a common ground for building a healthy academic culture for success.

Of course, the *energizing educator*, like everyone else, must find time to rest, reflect and replenish that energy. Certainly, the energy is replaced with evidence of student success on the obvious measures established by local, state and national entities. Reading educational research and *"thinking"* about how we can improve student academic success also energizes the psychological and emotional batteries. When those ideas are turned into classroom strategies and they positively impact learning, then this fission occurs as well.

There are so many pockets of *energizing educators* in your learning community who are making a positive difference in the success of our students. By observing them, you can be personally stimulated into action as well. I have actually observed whole campuses who practice this process from the symbolic frame and who build, nurture and hold each other accountable for the reason we exist as an organization: to ensure that every child that walks into our collective classrooms is academically successful. Thank you for being an *energizing educator* for students! It benefits you, your students and other staff members who recognize your commitment to excellence.

Leadership Application

LEADERSHIP TOOL: *This leadership tool is learning how to become an energizing educator. You are the catalyst for other teachers and staff members who need to feed off your energy.* You can help yourself and others by reading brief educational articles related to your field and sharing those ideas with other educators. Your influence when your professional learning community meetings are occurring can impact the atmosphere and keep staff focused on your academic goals. You energize by learning and growing as an educator.

LEADERSHIP REFLECTION: How would you rate yourself as an energizing educator on your campus? Do you feel like you are more of an encourager or have you become a discourager? Can you personally identify others on your campus that fit the model of an energizing educator? Do these educators seem like people that other people want to be around because of their ability to promote a positive atmosphere? Do they add to the culture of your campus?

LEADERSHIP APPLICATION: Be purposeful this week in being an energizing educator for someone on your campus. A good way to do this is to share an instructional activity that you have a track record of success with and know that others could benefit from it as well. Another way is to talk to another person about an educational article that you have read recently and share the components of the article that might be of benefit for students. Find a way to fill up the emotional tank of another staff member. You might even suggest a small study group on a particular topic of interest to you and others.

LEADERSHIP RESULTS: This is an important part of growing as an educator and as an instructional leader. Take a moment to enter your thoughts in the journal space (as suggested in the introduction) and take a few minutes to reflect on this week's application. Was the application successful? What were some indicators of success? What were the indicators of failure (this is important)? What can you do differently to improve on this particular leadership tool?

RESPONSE:

_____

_____

_____

_____

_____

LEADERSHIP SKILL SET: You are an energizing educator. This is not a skillset that will drain you of your personal emotional, mental, social and religious resources. When used properly, you help to stimulate encouraging classroom cultures in other parts of your campus and the response to those reactions serve as sources of encouragement for you. This is where the fission idea is applied. Part of the byproduct for your campus is a building of a culture of academic success, and you will have played a big part in that. In addition, people will enjoy being around you because they will leave you pumped and ready to go rather than feeling drained and lethargic. Make a difference!

But those who wait on the LORD
Shall renew *their* strength;
They shall mount up with wings like eagles,
They shall run and not be weary,
They shall walk and not faint.
Isaiah 40:31 NKJV

Lesson 10: Beliefs Bloom Behaviors

Students in criminology study the nature and causes of people who commit crimes, the behavior of criminals and the criminal-justice system. Criminologists work at understanding the belief and behavior systems of criminals to help predict and anticipate criminal behavior so they can avoid future law-breaking incidents and, in worse-case scenarios, catch the criminal(s) in the act. Criminologists understand that the established *beliefs bloom behaviors* of the criminal, and they use that information to catch and incarcerate them.

This is true for any micro or macro-system. Many organizations have stated values or a set of core beliefs, but in most cases, there is also an established set of unwritten practiced beliefs that are perpetuated by individuals or by the organization as a whole. A learning community such as yours is no different. A typical learning community that wants to focus on helping every student to achieve academic success must work individually and collectively to promote a culture that reinforces those beliefs. To do that we must continually talk about what kind of system where *beliefs bloom behaviors* which, in turn, creates a culture for student success.

One would think that the way we would change behaviors would be to change what we believe. In fact, it is quite the contrary. If our organization is going to truly accept the "attitude" that we are here to help every child achieve academic success, we must "behave" in a way that demonstrates the belief system we want to create. Therefore, the answer is change the behavior. *Act* in a way that says, "We believe," and look for success stories in student achievement. When you, your campus and the learning community begin to hear the stories of success, the belief system begins to change at the individual, grade level, subject area and at the campus and learning community level. Success is contagious. Success can create *beliefs that bloom behaviors*. Those behaviors then reinforce the desired student success.

Noel Tichey is a firm believer in telling the stories of success to help create a culture of success in an organization. Tichey[10] (2002) states that stories engage the people in the organization and the stories are the foundation for creating teamwork and energizing individuals to contribute to the ongoing success of the organization. Your campus has hundreds, if not thousands, of stories to tell related to student success and overcoming learning challenges and difficulties to achieve success. When we begin to share those stories with others and we must - we help establish the culture of success. We help to create *beliefs that bloom behaviors*.

Whose responsibility is it to change behaviors that create student success which, in turn, establishes a new belief system? It is mine; it is yours; it is everyone that touches the life of a student on your campus. If you are a teacher, you are a leader. It is not a choice; it is a responsibility. You are entrusted with the success of the students in your class. Each of us must be the difference-maker for our students at the classroom level, as campus administrators and as district personnel who come to work every day to educate our students. Classroom culture, campus culture and learning community culture matter...to our students. We must be firm in our commitment and create a culture in which our *beliefs bloom behaviors* that help every student to achieve success.

Leadership Application

LEADERSHIP TOOL: *The leadership tool that you are trying to develop and refine is your own personal belief system about student success. If you adjust your attitude about all students and their ability to learn and achieve success, then your behavior and your actions will follow accordingly.* The second part of this "blooming" process is to act upon it by sharing stories of success. You must begin to behave in a way that supports the belief system that supports academic success for all students.

LEADERSHIP REFLECTION: Are your own personal attitudes about student success aligned with your behaviors? Do you act in such a way that you truly believe that all of your students will achieve academic success? Do you take the time to share student success with the students themselves and with your colleagues? Think about the changes you may need to make internally so that student success can occur externally.

LEADERSHIP APPLICATION: Look for small success stories that have occurred in your classroom. Make sure that you make note of those. Be sure to include even the smallest successes. Those are the ones that will "bloom" into bigger and more obvious successes once they are watered. This week, when those student successes occur, stop the normal classroom activities and verbally highlight the success and the student(s). I would also suggest that the class as a whole recognize the student'(s) success with something simple with something like a one clap, two clap or a three clap response. You will be amazed at what it will do for that student receiving the recognition and the desire for others to want to excel as well. Make it a habit and watch successful student academic behavior begin to bloom.

LEADERSHIP RESULTS: This is an important part of growing as an educator and as an instructional leader. Take a moment to enter your thoughts in the journal space (as

suggested in the introduction) and take a few minutes to reflect on this week's application. Was the application successful? What were some indicators of success? What were the indicators of failure (this is important)? What can you do differently to improve on this particular leadership tool?

RESPONSE:

_____

_____

_____

_____

_____

LEADERSHIP SKILL SET: To develop this skill, you must conscientiously begin to evaluate your own personal behaviors and attitudes about student learning and academic success. Remember that to change your attitude, you must change your behavior. First, begin to act the way in which you believe your students will behave and respond. Then begin telling others the success stories, no matter how small those successes are at this point. They will begin to grow. It will become contagious in your classroom first, and then, on your campus.

Blessed is the man who trusts in the Lord, and whose hope is the Lord.

Jeremiah 17:7 NKJV

Lesson 11: Celebrating Stories of Success

I recently watched a video that had Steve Jobs, the co-founder of Apple, as the main speaker. Much of the video was centered on the newer version of the iPad; however; a portion of his time in front of his employees celebrated the company's many successes. It was inspiring to hear what the company had achieved over the past year. This global company took valuable time celebrating stories of success. I could feel the positive atmosphere among the employees and stockholders attending the meeting. What a great culture of success in that company!

Any organization that takes time *celebrating stories of success* understands the importance of that celebration as an investment in the future. For us, the investment translates into success for children. This type of celebration focuses on individual student success, which is the foundation of any educational organizational culture. It is not a celebration of leaps and bounds but incremental improvement by students who begin to have the proverbial light come on because teachers invested and reinvested time and resources to help make a difference in their lives.

Noel Tichey is considered one of the top writers both in leadership development and in helping to build winning organizations. Tichey[11] (2002) describes the importance of leaders and organizations telling their stories to help weave

66

together the ideas, values and models of behavior that an organization wants to demonstrate and emulate, as well as using stories to tell others "who we are" as an organization. Much of this type of success for our organization does not translate into noteworthy accomplishments that are reported in a state-mandated test that appears in a report. These are stories of success that every classroom teacher can share about several students in his/her class. They are improvements that appear small on the grand scheme of things but are huge in the life of that student and the teachers who work tirelessly to get there.

Celebrate stories of successes! Share the stories with the student, with the class, with your peers and with your campus. Tell the parents. Tell your neighbor. Tell the person in the shopping center the next time you are out and hear someone denigrating any education system. Educators make great strides with our students each and every day. We are in the greatest profession ever created and too often we hide our stories of success instead of sharing them.

Taking the time to tell our stories helps to create a culture of success. It also reinforces our culture of keeping the focus on our students and their successes. Keep up the good work and take time to tell others what good things are going on in our classrooms on a daily basis!

Leadership Application

LEADERSHIP TOOL: *The leadership tool that you are trying to develop is to learn how to tell the story of student success on a regular basis. The underlying principle of sharing stories of success is that you begin to develop a classroom, campus and even a learning community culture based on the aura of those stories.* Classroom teachers do not realize the potential impact that verbalizing student success has on the student and as important, the building of the classroom culture of success.

LEADERSHIP REFLECTION: How often do you verbally share with your students and colleagues the simple stories of success? Do you have students in your classroom who learn at a slower rate than others do, yet they are still progressing? What about the over achiever who people have grown to expect success? Does he continue to receive accolades from you, his teacher? Think about the ways and opportunities that you can celebrate stories of success in your classroom.

LEADERSHIP APPLICATION: Make a plan to identify several ways that you can celebrate your students' academic successes. That is a good place to start. When those moments occur, and they will, stop and share it with the whole class and make sure that you focus on the effort and the accomplishment while highlighting the idea that the student's success means the student is improving academically. The other students will begin to pick up on this phenomenon and will work to make their dreams come true as well. They will also want their teacher to publically recognize them. No matter how introvert the students may appear, we all love to be recognized for our accomplishments. If you are having a campus faculty meeting or a professional learning community meeting, take an opportunity to share a student's or some students' successes. It is not bragging. It is outlining your expectations of academic success for your students, and you have an opportunity to influence the culture or your campus. Other teachers will catch on and begin using this leadership tool.

LEADERSHIP RESULTS: This is an important part of growing as an educator and as an instructional leader. Take a moment to enter your thoughts in the journal space (as suggested in the introduction) and take a few minutes to reflect on this week's application. Was the application successful? What were some indicators of success? What were the indicators of failure (this is important)? What can you do differently to improve on this particular leadership tool?

RESPONSE:

_____

_____

_____

_____

_____

LEADERSHIP SKILL SET: To develop this skill, you must be determined to share and celebrate students' successes verbally. It takes a while to instill this type of skill set because we normally do not take the time to celebrate. There is usually too much stuff in the day's agenda to celebrate. However, if you try a dose of celebrating student success on a regular basis, your students will use this as fuel for learning. You are investing in your students and their academic success.

I can do all things through Christ who strengthens me.
Philippians 4:13 NKJV

Lesson 12: Conflict of Interest - Core Beliefs Colliding with High-Stakes Testing

I always loved going to the county fair when I was growing up. Every summer, the fairgrounds would fill up with all kinds of rides and amusement sideshows. The main walk of the midway would be full of people trying to entice fairgoers to spend money at their booths. We had very little money growing up. My mom did not work outside the home, and therefore, money was always tight, especially having four brothers. When I was old enough to venture out at the fair on my own, she gave me my portion of the tickets and reminded me several times that there would be no more money for the fair. I did not realize it at the time, but that was MY capital, which I could spend on the things that interested me. So, I chose carefully. I always left satisfied because although there were many rides and amusements that interested me, I chose to spend my capital, my money, on the things that interested me most!

Our education system can be compared to a huge fairground of learning opportunities. The challenge is that we have been given the tickets and told exactly where they have to be spent. It is on one assessment ride, and this ride is not very fun or amusing. This ride might be enjoyable and appropriate for some, but not for all. It presents a *conflict of interest.* We have so many other avenues in our repertoire of learning rides at our educational fair that we cannot use because of our narrowly defined assessments at the state and national levels. We cannot accurately, appropriately and adequately assess the whole student and his/her true mastery of learning because of the narrow assessment limits placed upon students through this assessment process.

The current state and national assessment systems create a conflict of interest for educators. It has never been about accountability, as some powerful business interest groups and lobbyists would have our citizens to believe. We have always believed accountability is necessary. What we do not want though is a dysfunctional accountability system that does not fairly and accurately measure the whole student for success.

It is time for us as an educational system to broaden our perspective on what we value as a community and as a state regarding those characteristics that identify students as being successful and prepared for success as independent individuals when they graduate. The current tendency is to focus on giftedness that is found in general intellectual ability, recognizing students who score higher than their peers on standardized testing. This indeed is a gift and should be recognized, but an entire learning community should not be held accountable for one single area of its students' abilities and giftedness.

Why do we not show the same consideration for achievement in the other areas of giftedness such as specific domains of academic aptitude or talent, creative and productive thinking, leadership ability, visual and performing arts and psychomotor ability, as identified by the National Society for the Gifted and Talented?[12] Any learning community's core beliefs would support a broader more holistic approach that provides a more accurate account of student success, but our mandated accountability system which demands a system of academia that focuses on all students graduating with the intent on enrolling into post-secondary education stifles such an inclusive process and creates a *conflict of interest*.

College was the best place for me, and most likely many of you, but is it the best place for everyone? Surely, with the technology that we have availed to us, we can devise an appropriate educational system that is more inclusive of the divergent aptitude gifts our students possess. We need to help our students begin to unwrap and embrace those gifts. Unfortunately, the narrowly defined focus of many of the state assessments, which target national norms, prohibit a more diverse assessment of our students' giftedness as described earlier and for the expertise those teachers possess to bring out those areas of giftedness.

We have begun to lose a generation of independent thinkers, idea generators, collaborative learners, extemporaneous writers, problem-solving leaders, artists, musicians, dancers, actors, carpenters, mechanics and other important contributors to our society due to the shortsightedness and undue focus on a narrowly defined set of academic standards. It is time to turn this *conflict of interest* around and begin to open up and recognize the vast array of assessment rides that are available to our students and encourage them to reinvest in the joy of learning in all areas of aptitude. We owe this much to our students and to ourselves. Thankfully, the capacity to do this exists within the walls of our classrooms and individual teacher leadership. Help your students find the best within themselves.

Leadership Application

LEADERSHIP TOOL: *The leadership tool that you are trying to develop here is fairly simple. It is more of a mindset that needs to be embraced. The leadership tool to develop is to understand that each student is an individual with unique learning gifts in one or more areas of aptitude.* You must be willing to broaden your concept of student success and allow for the areas of giftedness to blossom. Classroom teachers have been forced to focus on that narrow band of state and standardized assessments for so long that we have begun to ignore or failed to recognize that our students may be gifted in other areas. Keep your eyes open for other avenues of success.

LEADERSHIP REFLECTION: How often do you take a moment to step back and consider the ways students can demonstrate success? Think about the different kinds of aptitude in which students can demonstrate success? Have you considered the areas of creative and productive thinking, leadership ability, visual and performing arts and psychomotor ability? Is it possible that you have students who are struggling in your current discipline, but may be excelling in one of these areas? Think about the ways and opportunities that you can utilize these other areas to bring about success.

LEADERSHIP APPLICATION: We cannot ignore the current state and national accountability standards, toss them out the window and throw caution into the wind. However, we can use these hidden talents to our advantage. Consider some of the students in your classes who may be struggling. Think of some possible activities to capitalize on those strengths. Occasionally, when students experience success in one of the areas of aptitude, that sense of accomplishment and success can be carried over to another area of aptitude as well. You are capitalizing on that student's strength to find success in other areas. Make sure that when success occurs, you utilize the tool of celebrating success as well.

LEADERSHIP RESULTS: This is an important part of growing as an educator and as an instructional leader. Take a moment to enter your thoughts in the journal space (as suggested in the introduction) and take a few minutes to reflect on this week's application. Was the application successful? What were some indicators of success? What were the indicators of failure (this is important)? What can you do differently to improve on this particular leadership tool?

RESPONSE:

_____

_____

_____

_____

_____

LEADERSHIP SKILL SET: To develop this skill, you must be willing to invest some time in the less emphasized areas of aptitude. It may take a little while to gain a more comfortable understanding in these areas, but you can also create some incredible friendships and collaborative ideas by spending some time with other teachers in these lesser focused aptitudes like the band teacher, the choir teacher, the art teacher, the creative writing teacher and the coaches. Many coaches would love to team up with academic teachers who have a thirst for the knowledge and understanding of psychomotor skills. Once you become more familiar with the different areas of giftedness, your application of those skills in the classroom may turn a learning switch on in the areas of standardized assessment for one or more of your students.

Repay no one evil for evil. Have regard for good things in the sight of all men.
If it is possible, as much as depends on you, live peaceably with all men.
Romans 12:17-18 NKJV

Lesson 13: Decisions that Make a Difference

It was early in the morning on April 18, 1971. It was a foggy morning that begged for additional sleep, but it was not to be this morning as I was awakened from my sleep in our family home by a deafening noise. I was on the second floor of our tiny two story house, and I rushed down stairs only to learn that a small single propeller plane had clipped a tree in our front yard, skimmed over our roof and crashed in our back yard taking out the wire fence and rolled into a ball in a field about 75 yards behind our house. It was a Sunday morning. On Saturday night before the Sunday morning plane crash, my two best friends and I had planned to camp out in the field behind our house as we normally did on the weekends. However, for some reason, we had spent most of Saturday evening messing around and at the last minute we made a decision not to put up my dad's old army tent because it was past 10:30 p.m., and we were all too tired to make that much of an effort. As I surveyed the path of the plane's roll on the ground, I noticed that it had rolled right through the place where we usually camped out. I was convinced that the decision that we made the night before not to sleep in our tent most likely saved our lives. Albeit, unknowingly, it was definitely a *decision that made a difference*!

It is estimated that classroom teachers make an average of between 900 and 1,000 instructional decisions a day concerning the students and their classroom. It would be next to impossible to break down and analyze each and every decision classroom teachers make, but as a classroom observer, I know that teachers make lifesaving decisions for students all the time; *decisions that make a difference.* Most of the decisions teachers make are minor, but many of those decisions incorporate a larger perspective on individual and collective student achievement.

Many of the 900-1,000 decisions that are made each day about a child's education are not as important as the <u>basis</u> of those decisions. Those decisions based on individual and collective student achievement must be grounded in organizational core beliefs. Phillip Schlechty[13] (2002) states that our beliefs are statements in which one is willing to act. Do you have a sense of what you are learning community core beliefs are and are you willing to act on them?

Some of the many decisions teachers do make on a daily basis relate to the fundamental core belief that value children and their right to a high quality education. They are based on the belief all students <u>can</u> learn and focus on the *teaching-learning* process. Those kinds of effective decisions cannot be made without a solid consensus by all members of the learning community who truly believe all students can learn. When decisions are made based on your learning community's core beliefs and those beliefs are put into action, your learning community will prosper, but more importantly, your students will achieve greater academic success.

Leadership Application

LEADERSHIP TOOL: *This leadership tool is one of conviction and commitment. You must make a decision to identify why you do what you do. What core belief, what mantra are you willing to hang your educational shingle on and say I believe this within my heart of hearts about students and academic success?* This tool is a cornerstone builder for your innermost beliefs about teaching and student success. This should be an unshakeable belief. You must be able to bring personal clarity for yourself so that you can be strong and remain strong during those difficult decision-making times when others may be ready to abandon ship.

LEADERSHIP REFLECTION: What is it that you really believe about student learning and academic success? Do other teachers and faculty members believe and act in a manner that creates an atmosphere and culture which promotes high levels of expectation for student learning? Does your campus have a set of core beliefs that all educators accept and embrace? How can you positively influence your classroom and those around you for raising the level of

80

academic expectations on your campus and learning community?

LEADERSHIP APPLICATION: Think about what you really believe about your students and their learning expectations. Write down your current beliefs and actions you take in the classroom that either encourage or discourage student learning. Are there any changes you need to make? I would challenge you to visit your personal beliefs about student learning and consider raising your expectations for learning. They should be short, concise and clearly stated. Write those modified beliefs down as well. Here is the major application part. Verbalize your core beliefs to your students. If they are younger, state them in a way that they can understand your expectations. Call for a response from them. If they are old enough to respond in written form, ask them to do so and collect them once you have given them enough time to respond. You may find their responses enlightening and maybe even life-changing.

LEADERSHIP RESULTS: This is an important part of growing as an educator and as an instructional leader. Take a moment to enter your thoughts in the journal space (as suggested in the introduction) and take a few minutes to reflect on this week's application. Was the application successful? What were some indicators of success? What were the indicators of failure (this is important)? What can

you do differently to improve on this particular leadership tool?

RESPONSE:

_____

_____

_____

_____

_____

LEADERSHIP SKILL SET: To develop this skill, you must be willing to come to a personal and very real assessment about what you believe student learning is about for students. I would encourage you to stretch your learning expectations for students and give yourself the time to grow into it. It is amazing what students are willing to do for teachers who truly and honestly believe in them. Make a note to be observant with your students' responses to your verbalized belief statements that have been translated into applicable learning expectations and hopefully, raised expectations than what you previously believed. They just might become better students and through your own leadership, you may become a better teacher.

And if it seems evil to you to serve the LORD, choose for yourselves this day

whom you will serve, whether the gods which your

fathers served

that *were* on the other side of the River, or the gods of the

Amorites,

in whose land you dwell. But as for me and my house, we

will serve the LORD."

Joshua 24:15 NKJV

Lesson 14: Educational Heroes

I had the privilege of attending one of the annual opening ceremonies for the veterans who were a part of liberating the island of Iwo Jima from the Japanese during WWII. It was a very moving ceremony to be sitting in the room with men who were a part of what is recognized as one of the most ferocious battles to take place in the Pacific arena during WWII. Over six thousand men lost their lives to gain control of Iwo Jima, and they, as well as the survivors, represent and epitomize what it means to be a hero. The dwindling number of service men who risked their lives to liberate Iwo Jima gathers every year to remember those who did not return to American soil.

As they saluted our flag, it was easy to see on the faces and in the posture of these men that they love America and the freedoms for which America represents. The soldiers from the various military branches all shared a vision – to be victorious over the enemy. This shared vision, along with a shared set of common values and principles, helped them to overcome the tremendous odds at Iwo Jima and at battlegrounds all over the world.

The culture of any learning community must also share a set of common values and principles - a set of core beliefs that are not negotiated or compromised even under the most severe conditions or circumstances. The teachers and staff who refuse to accept defeat and defend these core beliefs are *educational heroes*. No, they do not sacrifice their lives, but they dedicate themselves for a lifetime to helping all students achieve academic success. These *educational heroes* recognize that to accomplish our educational mission, we can never waiver on these beliefs.

Teachers and staff must be unwilling to allow the *enemy* to get a foothold in their classrooms. Who and what is the *enemy*? It is those who would seek to devalue the importance of education and trivialize the impact it has on our nation and our society. It is complacency, apathy and defeatism. A culture that stands strong for holding students accountable for mastering learning and for refusing to accept less than the best produces students who have been released from the shackles of defeatism and who understand that failure is not final. These students move on to become productive lifelong citizens of a great community and nation. Teachers and staff who embrace this mantra and demonstrate it daily are *educational heroes*.

Educational heroes understand that to become a great learning community, we must be a culture of one. Lickona and Davidson[14] (2005) said it best when they said great schools row as one; they are quite clearly in the same boat, pulling in the same direction in unison. This does not mean that every individual in the learning community must be in lockstep unison but certainly must have the same set of learning expectations and values for all students.

These are schools with a common sense of purpose among the entire staff. These educators place their own personal agendas aside for the common good of the students, the school and the learning community in order for their students to demonstrate success. This type of self-sacrifice and collaboration produces *educational heroes*.

Though the challenges for education may appear to be overwhelming, the focus for us should remain on our students in the classroom. Our students will continue to achieve success because of the many *educational heroes* within our learning communities who will rise to the occasion. Thank you teachers, staff and administrators for what you do every single day to make a difference. You are our *educational heroes*.

Leadership Application

LEADERSHIP TOOL: *This leadership tool is one of developing the appropriate mindset not only for you, but also for your fellow teachers and staff members. What is the mindset for this leadership tool? It is to become sternly committed to student success at the highest levels possible.* This leadership tool must be developed through collaboration with other educators to achieve its fullest impact, but it has to start with you. You must decide that student success is a priority and envision that success for your students at the end of the year.

LEADERSHIP REFLECTION: What prohibits you from believing that all of your students can achieve academic success? Do you ever talk about what success looks like with other staff and faculty members? Do you believe your campus has the people who believe student success is possible? What behaviors do you need to change to begin making your classroom an incubator for student achievement?

LEADERSHIP APPLICATION: Talk to your students about the meaning of the words complacency, apathy and defeatism. Place those terms in the context of student achievement and pose questions to them that would identify the barriers to achieving academic success. Using the previous tools described in other leadership lessons, verbalize your high expectations and refusal to give in to failure. Verbally commit to your students and to campus staff that you are dedicated to your students' academic success, and you will not allow students to give up on themselves because you will never give up on them.

LEADERSHIP RESULTS: This is an important part of growing as an educator and as an instructional leader. Take a moment to enter your thoughts in the journal space (as

suggested in the introduction) and take a few minutes to reflect on this week's application. Was the application successful? What were some indicators of success? What were the indicators of failure (this is important)? What can you do differently to improve on this particular leadership tool?

RESPONSE:

_____

_____

_____

_____

_____

LEADERSHIP SKILL SET: To develop this skill of becoming an educational hero, determine and commit to never giving up on your students' academic successes, even when they give the impression of giving up. Many times, students give up so they can hide feelings of inadequacy and the fear of failure. When students realize that you are the safety net for them to fail, then they will sense it is okay to try more than once to succeed. If you are able to move toward this idea of helping all students achieve success, you begin to turn the tide against complacency, apathy and defeatism.

I beseech you therefore, brethren, by the mercies of God,

that you present your bodies a living sacrifice, holy, acceptable to God, *which is* your reasonable service.

Romans 12:1 NKJV

Lesson 15: Facing Our Fears

I love playing games with my grandchildren. They are still very young, but all of them went through this phase, as most children do, where they believe others cannot see them when they close their eyes. Of course, I played the proverbial hide-and-seek game using that motif. The kids would close their eyes, and I would pretend I could not find them until they opened their eyes, and we would enjoy some laughs until something else caught their attention.

As adults, we sometimes wish that we could close our eyes, and all of the concerns, troubles and fears would just vanish before we opened our eyes again. However, we learn to face our fears and work through them. Even more confounding is the fact that most of the issues we worry about never materialize, and most of the time we have very little control over the ones that actually do come to fruition.

Everyone has experienced fear in his or her own life at one time or another. Fear can be divided into two basic categories: healthy and unhealthy fear. On one hand, the healthy fear is the type of fear that teaches us as individuals to develop a conscious respect that keeps us from harming others and ourselves. It is a simple understanding that if one walks in front of a moving vehicle, serious physical harm could occur. It is understanding the laws of nature and man and adhering to those laws.

On the other hand, it is the unhealthy fears that we allow to burgeon in our minds to the point that we are unproductive and irrational in our thinking, and it begins to affect our efficiency. This type of fear is unproductive to the person and to the learning community. There are times in all of our lives that we need to step back and refocus so that we can *face our fears*. We can *face our fears* by replacing it with leadership courage. I read in a military article recently that stated, *"Personal courage isn't the absence of fear; rather, it's the ability to put fear aside and do what's necessary."* Therefore, in a sense, we never really eliminate that fear; we replace it with constructive and productive action.

Everyone in your learning community is called to perform specific duties and responsibilities. It seems like each year, each semester, and each week a new challenge faces you causing those fears to rematerialize. But, what I observe regularly in learning communities are custodians, cafeteria workers, maintenance men, paraprofessionals, teachers and administrators who are willing to step up and accept what Cotrell[15] (2004) refers to as a courageous leader who has the heart to do things which foster and support progress and accepts responsibility for those decisions.

No doubt, something new today or this week will trigger the anxiety that transforms into fear. We will *face our fears* with the courage in knowing that all of us will make decisions that keep student success in the forefront and as the reason we perform our responsibilities.

It all boils down to individually and collectively deciding to *face our fears* and whether we will continue to create and sustain a culture of student success. We can whine or we can shine. The choice is ours. As for me, I see a light in our learning communities because I notice staff at all levels keeping their focus on student achievement.

Leadership Application

LEADERSHIP TOOL: *This leadership tool is one of developing the ability of facing your fears of success as an educator and replacing that fear with leadership courage. The leadership tool is being able to utilize leadership courage in times of need.* When you have the proper set of educational values (leadership tool) and when those fearful times arise, you are able to step into that leadership courage realm and move forward with conviction. What are some of those fearful moments? It may be when you are confronted by an irate parent that does not have all of the information about a particular issue and wants to blame you for a problem that is unresolved. It may be that your campus administrator is uninformed about a project your students are doing and he/she is getting phone calls of concern. It may be that you are allowing students more than one opportunity to master the learning material and your fellow teachers are not on board with your philosophy about what student success really means to you.

LEADERSHIP REFLECTION: Very few people enjoy confrontations and controversy. Do you avoid doing the right thing and making right decisions about student achievement because you are fearful of the possible backlash that may occur? Are you always striving to stay under the radar so that you will not be singled out for good or bad? Is there a person on your campus that demonstrates a healthy measure of leadership courage, especially under fire? What behaviors do you need to change to begin demonstrating some measure of leadership courage?

LEADERSHIP APPLICATION: This particular application is not one that can necessarily be planned but more like being prepared for once the occasion arises. It would be best to take this topic to a professional learning community such as your grade level or subject level and ask your educator friends if they ever have a need to demonstrate leadership courage. Make a note of the occasions that they respond to and mentally prepare to do the same once your time comes.

LEADERSHIP RESULTS: This is an important part of growing as an educator and as an instructional leader. Take a moment to enter your thoughts in the journal space (as

suggested in the introduction) and take a few minutes to reflect on this week's application. Was the application successful? What were some indicators of success? What were the indicators of failure (this is important)? What can you do differently to improve on this particular leadership tool?

RESPONSE:

_____

_____

_____

_____

_____

LEADERSHIP SKILL SET: To develop this skill, this skill of leadership courage, be prepared for two things. First, understand that when you demonstrate conviction there will be a response. For every action, there is a reaction. You cannot control how other people act; you can only control how you react. Be prepared that for your commitment to leadership courage to do the right thing concerning your students and student achievement, you may receive some negative responses. Finally, and this is an important point, having leadership courage means having the courage to admit when you are wrong. A new piece of information may skew the entire picture, and as the educator, it takes leadership courage to say, "I was wrong." I have had more positive results from my personal experience when I have admitted to my students that I made a mistake. I suspect that you are much like me; you are human.

For the Spirit God gave us does not make us timid,
but gives us power, love and self-discipline.
2 Timothy 1:7 NKJV

Lesson 16: Fractal Leadership: Replicating Success

Many years ago during my doctoral studies, I became intrigued with one of our leadership class discussions. We were discussing repeating patterns called fractals that can be found both in the natural world and in the day-to-day lives of human behavior and existence. Fractals are simply reoccurring patterns. Fractals are found in measures of music put together to create a repetitive sound. Art finds fractals in tessellations, reoccurring patterns that create mosaics. Probably the most prevalent examples come from science. The fractal patterns in human biology can be seen as a significant part of the building blocks that sustain our existence.

How can the ideas of fractals be connected with a learning culture such as ours? It is this very pattern of *fractal leadership* that replicates success, which allows our culture of learning to continue to exist, survive and grow. Any entity, regardless of whether it is a living organism or an organized company, must realize the importance of the external factors that affect the operation of the organization and how each organization must adjust to those factors.

Our continued survival as a viable educational institution depends upon our ability to promote *fractal leadership* that replicates academic success. How does *fractal leadership* develop? It is in understanding that a successful learning culture values leadership development and creates opportunities for individuals to test their leadership skills at all levels of the organization. It is taking the components of a successful classroom, campus and learning community and replicating what is good about those entities. The development of *fractal leadership* begins with a process of connectivity with one another over a common bond of core beliefs. Replicating good leadership must begin with relationships. Wheatly[16] (1999) states that people need to be connected to the *identity* of the organization...connected to *new information*...and to be able to develop *relationships* with people anywhere in the system.

Developing *fractal leadership* is an essential component to creating a vibrant learning organization that values people who are willing to grow and accept responsibility for the educational organization's success. *Fractal leadership* leads to student academic success and creates a consistency of success for the culture. People who are willing to learn and to grow understand that their growth in replicating good leadership skills from others in the organization results in student success. The focus is and should always be student success, not just acquiring leadership skills.

Our learning communities are living, breathing organizations that are much like organisms – either growing or dying. Our learning community is in a constant state of change via the outside influences and the internal core beliefs. Those who are a part of the organizational culture who refuse to accept the external catalysts for change are doomed to affect the decline in student success. Staff members, who participate in the replication of leadership skills which promote increased student success, will struggle, stumble, participate in deep learning and grow as both an educator and as a fractal leader.

Let us support our *fractal leaders* who are replicating success and who are willing to take risks to increase student success. In that type of learning culture, students will acquire a sense of security in trying, and our individual staff members will develop as *fractal leaders* who promote student success. The result will be a stronger culture of learning for all, including the staff. After all, it is always about building a culture that promotes student success, and for that, we should be thankful.

Leadership Application

LEADERSHIP TOOL: *This leadership tool is fractal leadership, and you develop this tool by determining to make a conscious decision to develop as a leader. You develop as a leader by identifying critical leadership tools in your classroom and campus and developing those tools. Then, you*

mentor other staff members using those tools and skill sets.
You are in essence becoming a fractal leader because you are
sharing your leadership tools with one or more people. The
best case scenario would be to join a cohort of people who
are hearing the same message about leadership development.
True fractal leadership begins to take place.

LEADERSHIP REFLECTION: Do you notice any sense
of replicating leadership tools or skill sets with other staff
members? Does your learning community provide
opportunities for teachers and staff members to grow by
developing as leaders using a common set of leadership
tools? Are you in a position to be able to mentor another
person using the fractal leadership component?

LEADERSHIP APPLICATION: Okay, you do not have to
make a long term commitment on this one. Start slow and
see what happens. I would challenge you to either become a
part of a group of educators who are participating in
leadership growth (book studies, use of a leadership
curriculum or reading leadership articles and discussing
them) or select one other teacher that you know could use
some mentoring and would benefit from your leadership and
encouragement. Just take one of the leadership tools and skill
sets you have acquired and share it with that person. If
nothing else, a budding, more professional relationship with
that person may occur. Most likely though, you will begin to

grow as a fractal leader because someone else is replicating your leadership.

LEADERSHIP RESULTS: This is an important part of growing as an educator and as an instructional leader. Take a moment to enter your thoughts in the journal space (as suggested in the introduction) and take a few minutes to reflect on this week's application. Was the application successful? What were some indicators of success? What were the indicators of failure (this is important)? What can you do differently to improve on this particular leadership tool?

RESPONSE:

_____

_____

_____

_____

_____

LEADERSHIP SKILL SET: To develop this skill, it is not something that can be fully developed in a short period of time, because you are growing as the "teacher" while your fractal learning is growing as well. Allow yourself some leeway with the teaching/learning aspect of fractal leadership. The result will be that you will grow as a leader, and you may pass along some valuable leadership skills to a colleague as well. It is important that during this time when you are operating as a leader that you identify the best of those leadership skills in your leadership repertoire and replicate them through a series of learning opportunities.

And let us not grow weary while doing good,
for in due season we shall reap if we do not lose heart.
Galatians 6:9 NKJV

Lesson 17: Got Myelin?

One would think that as technologically advanced as our world has become, we would have the ability to be able to develop a comprehensive body of knowledge about the brain, its functions and its capabilities. The truth of the matter is that the more we learn about the human brain and its capabilities, the less we really comprehend about its nearly limitless functions. As recently as twenty years ago, brain researchers still maintained that brain intelligence was basically finite and that individuals were born with a certain amount of cognitive intelligence; we understood that to be accurate. Today, it is now widely accepted that we can affect the intelligence of an individual as much as one standard deviation, given the right circumstances and training as the teacher and the learner.

One such discovery about the brain concerns a neuron insulating component referred to as *myelin*. Researchers have known about it for years but have never really understood its connection to improving intelligence until recent years. What is *myelin*? Coyle[17] (2009) shares that *myelin* is an insulator that wraps the neuron fibers used to send messages from one brain cell to another. So why should that information matter to teachers and other educators? These neuron paths are the support for the brain's super highways that transport knowledge and information from one cell to another.

Myelin is the insulator for the neuron paths. A significant aspect of *myelin* is that it is created through the practice of deep learning that occurs when the brain is authentically engaged in a challenging task. The more a student is engaged in deep practice, the more *myelin* is created, which in turn strengthens the neuropaths along which information travels allowing the student to become more proficient in that area of study.

Simply put, *myelin* helps the person develop and retain a skill through deep practice. The deeper the practice over time, the more *myelin* insulation is created. The outcome results in faster transportation of the neuron impulse to the receiving cells. The end result is growth in knowledge and in the skill needed to complete a task regardless of whether it is a mental or physical activity.

So, how does this information translate into useful application for the teacher and any student in the classroom? According to Doyle[18] (2009), *myelin* is universal, it is indiscriminant and it is imperceptible. Everyone grows it; it can be applied to any skill needed to be learned, and we cannot see it or feel it. We can only sense it because it reveals itself in improved skill building performance. When *myelin* is grown, it wraps itself around the neurons to be used to serve as insulation and provides a tighter, sharper, crisper response to the transmission of performance and information. It becomes, in effect, our brain's super highway for informational travel.

The classroom is the instructional ground to produce *myelin*. It is the learning lab to help students engage in deep practice to produce *myelin,* to produce skills, to produce results. We help to prepare for deep learning when we teach students the power of this physiological transformation that takes place by explaining to them what *myelin* does and that everyone can produce as much *myelin* as they can make through genuine deep learning. Does practice make perfect? No, but studies are beginning to show that practice does indeed make permanent. You are free to grow!

Leadership Application

LEADERSHIP TOOL: *To develop this leadership tool of growing myelin, it is important to understand that you will need to provide time for your students to engage in deep learning. It was not discussed at length in the learning lesson, but deep learning really takes place when the student is so engaged in his/her activity that he/she is not aware of his/her surroundings.* It is the type of learning that takes place when a student is in the "reading flow" and does not notice anything else because the student is so focused on the reading material. It is also characterized as short bursts of learning. This type of deep learning comes in segments. The more segments that you can link together with brief intervals in between, the greater amount of deep learning will take place. This can be a mental or physical activity, but it also can be both at the same time.

LEADERSHIP REFLECTION: Do you provide time for your students to engage in authentic deep learning? Is most of your class period taken by a stand and deliver approach with little opportunity for learning practice? Have you ever discussed the physiological aspect of the learning process with your students or with your professional learning community and how the knowledge of this process can have a positive effect on your students and their learning?

LEADERSHIP APPLICATION: To apply this tool of implementing the myelin deep learning, consider your own classroom(s) for a moment and determine if there are ways you can provide for more deep learning opportunities. Take a few moments to make sure you understand the importance of deep learning and how you can communicate the information of that process to your students. The "light bulb moment" for the students should be that myelin can be created by all students and is created by determined focused work of the student. Teachers, you cannot create myelin for them. Create this atmosphere for deep learning and try it once. Then, get some responses from your students.

LEADERSHIP RESULTS: This is an important part of growing as an educator and as an instructional leader. Take a moment to enter your thoughts in the journal space (as suggested in the introduction) and take a few minutes to reflect on this week's application. Was the application successful? What were some indicators of success? What were the indicators of failure (this is important)? What can you do differently to improve on this particular leadership tool?

RESPONSE:

_____

_____

_____

_____

_____

LEADERSHIP SKILL SET: To use deep learning on a daily basis, you must be purposeful in your planning. That means you may need to combine this skillset with another skillset discussed in this book of lessons by implementing some flipped learning so that you can find more time for the deep learning in your class. This is a difficult process to judge because you cannot look into the physiological minds of your students to see the myelin being created, but you will be able to see its results over a period of time. It is important that you maintain the vigil of providing time for deep learning processes to take place daily, if possible. It is always best to isolate a specific skill or piece of knowledge that you want the student to learning and then pulverize the knowledge with this deep learning process. Band teachers, choir teachers and coaches probably already do this and do not realize that this is what is happening within the minds of their students. A word of caution with this is that you do not "drill and kill" your students. Death by worksheets does not produce deep learning. It creates classroom exasperation and boredom for attending class.

For You formed my inward parts;
You covered me in my mother's womb.
[14] I will praise You, for I am fearfully *and* wonderfully
made;
Marvelous are Your works,
And *that* my soul knows very well.
[15] My frame was not hidden from You,
When I was made in secret,
***And* skillfully wrought in the lowest parts of the earth.**
[16] Your eyes saw my substance, being yet unformed.
And in Your book they all were written,
The days fashioned for me,
When *as yet there were* none of them.
Psalm 139:13-16 NKJV

Lesson 18: Guiding Students to Choose a Path of Destiny

I can remember the conversation as if it was yesterday. It was during my junior year in high school, and one of the football coaches offered me a ride back to our main campus from our workout center where I had just finished basketball practice. He abruptly explained to me that I was not going to be able to make a living playing professional basketball, so he asked me what I was really going to do to make something of myself in life. The truth is I was hurt by his comments. I was not hurt because he was more direct than I thought he should be, but because deep down, I knew in my heart of hearts that he was right. I did not appreciate his words or his direct demeanor at the time, but he did cause me to really contemplate what I was going to do with my future, and he forced me to look at other options. This coach took the time out of his schedule to help guide me to choose my *destiny*.

This football coach, who gave me a ride, was never a coach of mine, yet his words and his redirection had an impact on my personal *destiny*. He did not have to know everything about me; he just knew enough. He was an observer. Basketball helped to pay for most of my college, but it did not make a living for me. There would have to be something else for me to make a living.

We are educators. We are in a position of influence with every student we meet.

The greatest impact we have on students may not be the specific discipline we teach in class during the school year. Our greatest impact may be the few sentences of encouragement to the student who demonstrates giftedness in another area but has never been recognized for it. Each one of us has an opportunity every day to help students choose a *path of destiny*.

Truthfully, guidance in helping students choose their *path of destiny* is a form of motivation. Hawkins[19] (1994) refers to motivation as the key to helping students succeed in school. He states that when students know educators and parents believe in them and have high expectations, they are lifted up. We should take advantage of those opportunities to help students see what they can be good at and help guide them to choose a *path of destiny*.

We must be careful about unknowingly closing the doors of opportunity for a student without opening another door for them. When we limit opportunities for student success, we increase the chances for student failure and dropouts. We would be grossly negligent to indicate to a student that his/her only chance for destiny is through athletics or by becoming the next American Idol winner. Honestly, we are "key keepers" and we have a huge ring of keys. Our ring of keys contains at least one for each student we meet, and this key is to be used to unlock his/her potential for success in some area of giftedness. It is our challenge to find the right "key" to help each child choose his/her *path of destiny*.

No student has just one opportunity or a limited opportunity to choose a *path of destiny*. Granted, not everyone will be a star athlete, a professional dancer, an artist, a singer, a writer, a composer, a college graduate or even a teacher. Nevertheless, some will. Your challenge is to know your students well enough that you can help to guide them to their successful endeavors.

Use your talents as a teacher to motivate our students in such a way that when one door is closed another door is opened. Maybe, just maybe, you will be the influence in that student's life that makes a lifelong difference. Isn't that what educators do? Take your set of keys and start unlocking the potential in your students!

Leadership Application

LEADERSHIP TOOL: *This particular tool is more of a coaching tool. You are a destiny coach. If you have ever spent any time around coaching, good coaches do not just begin assigning students to play a particular position; they evaluate the student's strengths and weakness and capitalize* *on the student's strengths.* Therefore, you are going to become more of a focused observer and begin to develop skills on identifying your students' strengths and weakness so you can become an encourager for those areas of strength. It requires some patience and some time to become proficient, and then, remember that you are a guide, not the final say.

LEADERSHIP REFLECTION: Do you ever provide time to evaluate your students as a whole person and not just a student in the class of a particular discipline you are teaching? Do you ever recognize other areas of potential success in your students that do not necessarily coincide with your discipline? Do you know your students' real interests and what grabs their attention?

LEADERSHIP APPLICATION: This week's leadership application will require you to interact with another adult. Identify a choir teacher, an art teacher, a band teacher or a coach, other than yourself, and ask that person to share with you how they are able to identify students' strengths and talents. Make a note of what processes they use to complete their assessments of students. Ask the teacher if he/she has ever misplaced, overestimate or underestimated a student's talents. Record those results as well. Determine if any of their processes can be replicated and transferred to your area or discipline. Your objective here is to become more observant and to help students see their own potential, not just in your area of expertise, but in other areas as well.

LEADERSHIP RESULTS: This is an important part of growing as an educator and as an instructional leader. Take a moment to enter your thoughts in the journal space (as suggested in the introduction) and take a few minutes to reflect on this week's application. Was the application successful? What were some indicators of success? What were the indicators of failure (this is important)? What can you do differently to improve on this particular leadership tool?

RESPONSE:

_____

_____

_____

_____

_____

LEADERSHIP SKILL SET: This skillset is to develop yourself as a "coach" in the area of helping students to see where their potential skills are manifested and to help them to develop those to the best of their potential. You are an educator, and one of your responsibilities as an educator is to be a guide for your students. We live in an ever-expanding world of opportunities and as teachers we must accept

responsibility to guide our students to their path of destiny.
You light the way for them.

For I know the thoughts that I think toward you, says the
LORD,
thoughts of peace and not of evil, to give you a future and
a hope.
Jeremiah 29:11 NKJV

Lesson 19: Just Imagine

Just imagine participating in the Olympics, and you are at the starting line of the 100-meter dash. The objective for the race is to finish and to be the first one across the line because, by nature, a race is a competition. The continuum for running the race is time. The measure for success in this race is to compare all participants against the time continuum to determine the winner and the losers based on who finished first.

Now, *just imagine* yourself as a student in a core area subject classroom. What is the objective of this event? What is the continuum? A student who has been in a traditional education system might answer the first question by saying that the objective of the course is to learn the information correctly the first time because time, getting it right the first try and the number of attempts all make a difference in your final grade. The continuum in this is time as well. If you do not get it right the first time, then you are deemed less academically capable and assessed accordingly. Rather than making learning a race in education, *just imagine* if we decided that the objective is to provide everyone the opportunity to be a winner by getting everyone across the instructional finish line. The continuum then changes from focusing on <u>when</u> the student mastered the information to focusing on <u>that</u> the student <u>learned</u> it.

Just imagine if we viewed academic mistakes made by students as part of the learning process moving toward a better understanding of the material rather than a detrimental decision by the student that converts into influencing the final grade, incorrectly reflecting the student's true knowledge of the subject matter. Intuitive teachers, who are focused on helping all students achieve academic success, use these miscues to take a proactive approach in helping the student reach the ultimate finish line in the learning continuum. It seems reasonable that our profession take a more serious look at how we view the learning process and more importantly, the process of how we assess student learning. Should time matter or should mastery be the major focus?

Performance-based learning and assessment prescribes that educators examine the entire learning continuum with an emphasis on the finish line of learning. The question that teachers must ask is, "Did the student master learning the information?" We want to muddy the process of assessment by trying to place it on a time continuum and somehow equate that with a fairness grade with respect to other students. That is a bias that we have bought into as a profession because we have been taught in our own learning process that somehow it is unfair to the student who learned it during the first attempt if we deem another student successful when it took the other student multiple attempts to get to the same point in the learning continuum.

Somewhere in our pedagogy we have been led to believe that when students do not do the work or complete it well below the mastery rate, we teach our students to become accountable by assigning low or failing grades to them. Douglas Reeves[20] (2009) comments that over 90 years of research evidence has proven the contrary to this practice. So then, by focusing on performance-based learning, we require the students to complete the learning continuum and get to the academic finish line. The consequence of substandard work or incomplete work must be to require the student to complete the task until he/she has demonstrated mastery.

A learning culture that focuses on student success does not change from the top down. It most likely changes from the bottom up when there is a prevalence of leadership in the classroom. A true sustaining academic culture that focuses on learning rather than the process, changes from the inside out. It changes by one individual who places more importance on the product rather than the process in the classroom and by an individual who understands that performance-based learning is a process where learning is the objective. *Just imagine* the possibilities.

Leadership Application

LEADERSHIP TOOL: *This leadership tool is that of changing your personal mindset about student success and learning over time. If you believe that student accomplishments must be diminished if they do not master the material the first time, then I would encourage you to rethink your position on this before tackling this leadership tool.* Learning is the continuum and it takes students differing amounts of time to reach the expected goal. Our traditional educational system arbitrarily places the gifted student and the more learning challenged students in a time continuum and expects the same results at the same time. That is not only unfair to students, but to the teacher as well. Students learn at different rates.

LEADERSHIP REFLECTION: Do you expect all students to master the same amount of information at the same time? Does your campus culture breed expectations for students where they are denied the same academic rewards for not achieving the same results at the same time? Do you have students who are struggling, but deep down you know they could make it with a little more time?

LEADERSHIP APPLICATION: Take a moment to think about the segment of your classroom student population who are just missing the mark. Discuss with another colleague to see if there is a way that you can find some additional time for students to master the material. Here is a suggestion. If a student falls short on an assignment, instead of assigning a grade to the paper, require the student to go back and make the corrections and expect the student to explain the reason for the changes in the assignment. If the student can demonstrate that he/she has mastered the material, then give the student credit for mastery.

LEADERSHIP RESULTS: This is an important part of growing as an educator and as an instructional leader. Take a moment to enter your thoughts in the journal space (as suggested in the introduction) and take a few minutes to reflect on this week's application. Was the application successful? What were some indicators of success? What were the indicators of failure (this is important)? What can you do differently to improve on this particular leadership tool?

RESPONSE:

_____

_____

_____

_____

_____

LEADERSHIP SKILL SET: You are developing a skillset that is focusing more on WHAT the student is mastering rather than WHEN the student is mastering the information. This is one of the resisting paradigm shifts that may need to take place in your personal teaching repertoire before you can become more comfortable in this leadership skillset. There are many educators, and you may be one of them, that just struggle with this idea of fairness. Johnny got it the first time, so it is not fair that the other learners should be allowed additional chances at learning. If that is your philosophy in your heart of hearts, then I would suggest that you rethink your philosophy of education and what you believe teaching is really about with regard to student success. If you can give yourself a little grace in this area and *just imagine* what the potential is for struggling students, then this might just click for you.

This Book of the Law shall not depart from your mouth, but you shall meditate in it day and night, that you may observe to do according to all that is written in it. For then you will make your way prosperous, and then you will have good success. Joshua 1:8 NKJV

Lesson 20: Resolutions with Resolve (A New Year's Lesson!)

The beginning of a new calendar year always brings about those fateful New Year's resolutions that tend to be broken before the end of the first week. If you are one of those who are *really* committed, you may make it to the end of the month. Then, the depression sets in. Typically, by the end of the third week of January and certainly by the end of the month, there are usually more broken resolutions than those kept. Yuk!

Educators are certainly not immune to the results of unfulfilled resolutions, bills, and yes, the weather. Each spring shapes up to be challenging with the looming accountability assessments at the local and state levels that will be applied to your national evaluation. Additionally, changes that generally occur in curriculum each spring, and the new challenges that all learning communities face with the predicted shortfalls in funding add to the pressures of achieving our fundamental goals of academic mastery for all children. However, I do believe teachers have a steel resolve to push through the doldrums created by New Year's blues and those looming assessments to make the best of it. When directly connecting resolutions with education, the difference is *resolutions with resolve*!

Unlike businesses, educators do not create a product per se; we change lives!

Resolutions with resolve are those undeniable and uncompromising beliefs about our self and educating students. The *"resolve"* part of a resolution is to determine or come to a definite decision about students and learning. We must be unwavering in our commitment to educate students in the face of instructional adversities.

To be that determined and to *resolve* to meet those commitments, educators must be engaged in a type of leadership that Burns[21] (1978) calls transforming leadership. It is a type of *resolve* that engages others to want to follow others to a higher level of motivation and success. Here are a few resolutions for all educators to keep using that steel *resolve* for the sake of the students we serve:

- Keep the main thing, the main thing. Student success must be the focus.
  Do not give up on your students or yourself. They need you to believe in them.
- Collaboration. No one person is smarter than the whole. Utilize your professional learning communities.
- Keep learning. Your students will always follow your lead as a learner. Read or learn about something that will add to your current challenges as an educator.

- YOU be the positive influence. Naysayers will always want the floor. YOU be the one who makes a positive difference in meetings and your professional learning community. Too many good things are happening on your campus to allow them to slip by unnoticed.

- Keep your expectations for students high. Students will only achieve what you expect them to achieve. Do not forget to provide them with the support and resources they need as well.

- Give yourself and others grace. When you are trying to do the right things for students, it is okay when it does not always come together. Being a risk taker means that sometimes those strategies that look good on paper just do not produce the desired results. Do not give up!

Educators are generally a very committed and determined group. Thank you for your *resolve* to help students achieve success! It will be YOU that will make a difference in the lives of our students this spring.

Leadership Application

LEADERSHIP TOOL: *This leadership tool is developing the capacity of resolve. You must be unwavering in your commitment to educating all of your students.* To do this you must use some systemic thinking and be prepared for those natural roadblocks that tend to want to disrupt the learning process, especially during the spring when you are trying to bring the learning all together in preparation for the accountability assessments your state will be administering.

LEADERSHIP REFLECTION: Are you focused on every student being prepared to master their learning objectives? Are you allowing distractors to occupy your time that should be devoted to learning the critical objectives? Have you given up on one or more of your students? Does your campus make learning a priority and does the campus administration work to protect the learning time for students and for you? Are you highlighting student success?

LEADERSHIP APPLICATION: Make yourself a learning resolution list. Include in the list, the ideas and philosophies that were mentioned in the lesson above. Share your resolution with at least one other person on your campus. If you are really brave, share it with your professional learning community group and ask them to hold you accountable. That will do two things: first, it will make you more determined to meet your academic resolutions for your students, and it will also encourage your professional colleagues to think about redoubling their efforts for student success.

LEADERSHIP RESULTS: This is an important part of growing as an educator and as an instructional leader. Take a moment to enter your thoughts in the journal space (as suggested in the introduction) and take a few minutes to reflect on this week's application. Was the application successful? What were some indicators of success? What were the indicators of failure (this is important)? What can you do differently to improve on this particular leadership tool?

RESPONSE:

_____

_____

_____

_____

_____

LEADERSHIP SKILL SET: You are adding to your leadership tools the skillset of resolve. Resolve is a mindset that fewer and fewer of our educators possess. So many distractions can occur with local policies, state mandates, administrator personal preferences and not to mention parent concerns that arise throughout the year. You have to be the instructional watchmen, the gatekeeper and the classroom watchdog that resolves to keep the instructional time focused on instruction. Most importantly, you be the lifelong learner and commit to staying informed and continuing to grow by doing such things as reading and completing the lesson applications in this book!

The Lord is not slack concerning *His* promise, as some
count slackness,
but is longsuffering toward us, not willing that any
should perish but that all should come to repentance.
2 Peter 3:9 NKJV

Lesson 21: Frames of Cognition - The Structural Frame

During my doctoral work years ago, I became very interested in the work of educational researchers Lee Bolman and Terrance Deal on the *frames of cognition* and how this concept related to identifying leadership and leadership development. I must admit that most of my interest was perked out of the idea that these two researchers took a nebulous and abstract concept such as leadership, and they added tangible, doable characteristics for improving individual leadership through these identifiable concepts called *frames of cognition.*

Cognition can be defined as the process in which we perform mental tasks and steps to arrive at a solution or decision based on our prior knowledge of an event or series of events. It is the process of thinking about thinking and making some sense of our world around us. This all may sound a bit dreary and boring except for the fact that these *frames of cognition* are a part of the leadership characteristics we should all aspire to possess in an educational learning community, and they should be included in our repertoire of exemplary performance and leadership skills as educators in the classroom.

Bolman and Deal[22] (1997) have identified the four frames of cognition as the *structural frame*, the human resource frame, the political frame and the symbolic frame. I want to talk first on the *structural frame* and how it can impact our classrooms. The *structural frame* focuses on designing a pattern of roles and relationships that will accomplish collective goals and accommodate individual differences. That means if our learning culture is to exist successfully, we must have clear and efficient job responsibilities and tasks appropriately assigned for each member to perform his/her function. We must be effective at getting the job done according to expectations both in the classroom and throughout the learning community. We must have clearly established rules and routines while taking care of the mundane paperwork that always accompanies a viable and successful organization. These are the types of tasks that are not noticed when done properly but become glaringly apparent when not executed as expected.

The educator in the classroom must have mastery of the *structural frame of cognition* because our students are conditioned to learn to <u>read</u> the teacher in the classroom regarding his/her do's and don'ts. There must be some consistent form of structure in the classroom to provide a sense of orderliness and security so that our students can routinely catalogue and file our classroom expectations into that daily routine and move on to focusing on the learning that should take place. When a classroom teacher does not or cannot formulate consistent and fair *structural frame* processes for the students, a form of chaos occurs, and thus, the classroom becomes disorderly and possibly unmanageable. The resulting outcome is a classroom full of students who are focusing more on what the clear expectations are to be for the classroom rather than focusing their attention on academic learning.

Any learning community, whether that is the classroom, the campus or the entire learning community that has a focus on improving student achievement must have its members understanding the role of the *structural frame* in the classroom and use it to promote a positive healthy learning environment. Thank you to those teachers, staff members and administrators who are doing just that.

Leadership Application

LEADERSHIP TOOL: *This leadership tool is the structural frame of cognition. A teacher leader must have an understanding of the need for clarity in the structural frame. Acquiring this tool and using it to its fullest will promote a healthy safe and secure learning environment for your students.* You must be willing to invest some time in evaluating your classroom management rules and regulations, as well as your campus and learning community expectations for maintaining structure and cohesive procedures within the walls of your classroom.

LEADERSHIP REFLECTION: Do you consider that your current classroom management procedures are adequate for maintaining both orderliness and security for your students? Do you remain open to the possibilities for improving the structure in your classroom? Are you cooperative and dependable when it comes to maintaining and turning in required records and documents for your campus and the learning community? Do you seek ways to improve the efficiencies of your current job responsibilities and offer ideas to others for improvement?

LEADERSHIP APPLICATION: Take the time to review your personal classroom management responsibilities with regard to your rules and regulations. Are they simple enough for students to comprehend and follow, and do they adhere to the guidelines set forth by your campus administrators as well as the learning community? Review your last six-week's responses to your campus's office requirements and expectations for turning in required paperwork such as grades and attendance information. Evaluate your response based on whether you have complied in the time frame established by your campus. Consider revising and making the necessary changes to comply with campus regulations and make suggestions for improvement in the appropriate manner if you develop any ideas for the campus as a whole.

LEADERSHIP RESULTS: This is an important part of growing as an educator and as an instructional leader. Take a moment to enter your thoughts in the journal space (as suggested in the introduction) and take a few minutes to reflect on this week's application. Was the application successful? What were some indicators of success? What were the indicators of failure (this is important)? What can you do differently to improve on this particular leadership tool?

RESPONSE:

_____

_____

_____

_____

_____

LEADERSHIP SKILL SET: This skill set of being able to operate efficiently out of the structural frame is one of the unrecognizable and unrewarded skill sets when done properly, but it is also one of the more noticeable skill sets when it is not adhered to according to your campus and learning community expectations. In some extreme cases, legal ramifications could occur if blatant neglect is suspected or occurs. Developing this skill set requires attentiveness to the details. It may be necessary to establish a "to do" list or a "tickle file" and use those reminders to complete the necessary paperwork that must be turned in by a specific time period. Developing the structural frame may also mean some time will be necessary for you to reflect periodically on the classroom atmosphere and on student safety. Complacency can become the deceiver for a safe and orderly environment. A good handle on the structural frame allows you to redirect your attention back on instruction.

Therefore comfort each other and edify one another, just as you also are doing.
I Thessalonians 5:11 NKJV

Lesson 22: Frames of Cognition - The Human Resource Frame

My fondest memories of my teachers going through education were not necessarily that they were good teachers, which most of them were. I remember them because of the sincere interest they took in me. I am talking about the teachers who would talk to me about something that I said in a previous class or spoke to me about something that was specific and unique about me. That seems a bit self-centered, but the truth is, we all enjoy being recognized as a unique person with individual qualities that others see in us. I did not realize it at the time, but these teachers were capitalizing on the attributes of the *human resource frame* of cognition. They were seeking information from me or stating information to me that reinforced the unique individuality of my person. They valued me as a unique individual.

Bolman and Deal[23] (1997) stated that the *human resource frame* highlights the importance of needs and motives. Organizations work best when individual needs are met, and the organization provides a caring, trusting, work environment. This is true for relationships between employees in the organization, as well as those relationships between the employees and the students. Care and trust are qualities that are built over time, and when a teacher has the opportunity to see the same students every day, then the attributes of the *human resource frame* can be nurtured. This process is the nourishment needed for academic growth.

Extraordinary teachers who want to develop their leadership skills understand the importance of utilizing the frame of cognition referred to as the *human resource frame* to build healthy relationships with their students. This idea of building relationships with students, while in the midst of a standards-based accountability system, exemplifies the need to utilize the *human resource frame* to help our students achieve academic success. We all have an innate desire for self-worth and acceptance. Exceptional teachers use the *human resource frame* to connect with the student so that additional and greater opportunities for learning can take place inside and outside of the classroom.

This is a part of the learning process that will not be found in commercially developed lesson plans or academic objectives. The *human resource frame* is an attribute found in the art of teaching that a skillful teacher selects from his/her repertoire of teaching tools and skills to make that connection between the teacher and the student, which in turn allows a greater desire on the part of the student to want to succeed.

Although it can be viewed as a form of extrinsic motivation, this connection can also be used to create within the student the understanding for the need to learn, therefore, transferring the process from extrinsically motivated to intrinsically motivated learning. The outcome of becoming proficient in using the *human resource frame* is improved student achievement while reinforcing the individual self-worth of the student. Not a bad combination of relationship building ingredients for student success.

If you are seeking to improve your leadership skills or if you just want to become a better teacher, think upon the attributes of the *human resource frame* and how you can positively influence your co-workers and your students. Be the change agent for student success by investing a little more time in the *human resource frame*. The result will be improved student achievement and the students holding you in high regard. And that is as it should be.

Leadership Application

LEADERSHIP TOOL: *This leadership tool is the human resource frame of cognition. You must consciously work at developing this particular tool to be effective. Acquiring this tool and using it to its fullest will promote healthy and professional relationships with your students and other staff members.* It takes a concerted effort on your part to begin intentionally building those relationships because you want to see the outcome, which is culminated though improved student academic performance, as well as a raised measure of respect for you personally.

LEADERSHIP REFLECTION: Do you conscientiously stop and take the time to give your students the attention they are asking for when they address you? Do you apply the verbal and physical cues such as responding to their comments, giving direct eye contact and demonstrating attentive body language when a student or a group of students are speaking to you? Do you give the time on occasion to give students of your time outside the classroom by attending students' extra or co-curricular activities? Do the students appreciate your presence in and out of the classroom?

LEADERSHIP APPLICATION: Conscientiously evaluate your posture and verbal comments to students when they are speaking to you. Make an effort to reply to them by repeating the critical aspects of their conversations to you when they are speaking to you. Evaluate your calendar to determine if you can possibly attend some of your students' activities outside the classroom and if it is possible for you to do so. Afterwards, make positive and encouraging comments about those students when they are in your class after you have attended their activities. Sometimes, even a note to the student's parent(s) or guardian complimenting the student's performance in class can also serve as a catalyst for developing healthy relationships. **LEADERSHIP RESULTS**: This is an important part of growing as an educator and as an instructional leader. Take a moment to enter your thoughts in the journal space (as suggested in the introduction) and take a few minutes to reflect on this week's application. Was the application successful? What were some indicators of success? What were the indicators of failure (this is important)? What can you do differently to improve on this particular leadership tool?

RESPONSE:

_____

_____

_____

_____

_____

LEADERSHIP SKILL SET: This skill set can be one of the more rewarding skill sets that you develop. If not carefully monitored, it can also become your downfall as well. It is a powerful cognitive frame with potentially very satisfying rewards through the funnel of improved student success. It is important to be diligent not to allow yourself to cross the line with regard to professional behavior and appropriate expectations. Understanding the essence and the power of the frame is the key to utilizing its potential. The personal rewards for the teacher can become very satisfying through improved student achievement as well as students and staff holding you in high esteem and regard. Just do not forget that the purpose for building <u>healthy</u> relationships is to improve student academic achievement. In doing this, you will make significant academic strides with your students.

A new commandment I give to you, that you love one another;
as I have loved you, that you also love one another.
By this all will know that you are My disciples,
if you have love for one another.
John 13:34-35 NKJV

Lesson 23: Frames of Cognition - The Political Frame

If you were like me and fortunate enough to have had more than one guardian growing up, you were guilty of this as a child. When you did not like the answer that you received from one parent, you probably tried the other. Of course, it never took too long for my parents to catch on. I had to figure out a different plan of attack to get my way, but I was always devising and making plans to see if there was a way to get what I wanted. In its simplest form, I was utilizing what Bolman and Deal referred to as *the political frame*. I was utilizing my available resources to acquire more resources.

There are politics at play in every organization; whether it is a company, a social group, a church affiliation or even a family, *the political frame* is at work. It is not deviant behavior or some backroom form of decision-making. It is a legitimate part of the human structure to vie for the limited resources that are available. It is the political aspect of supply and demand. Bolman and Deal[24] (1997) point out the limits of authority and the inevitability that resources will be scarce to fulfill all demands placed upon the organization. Does that sound familiar? Not enough resources to go around for everyone is a common theme throughout all human groups and associations. It is important for individuals in a learning organization to recognize the *political frame* as real and operational, not as a stumbling block or as an excuse for failure.

Really understanding this *political frame*, its limitations and the value it can bring, from the classroom teacher to the superintendent of the learning organization, is vital. The classroom teachers must be able to mobilize their resources and the people they have at their disposal. Educators must be able to utilize their persuasive and influencing skills to bring any and all resources available to use in helping students achieve success.

Classroom teachers are also very effective in mustering support and cooperation for the resources and tools they need to help students. In addition, most teachers are adroit in developing and securing support beyond the bounds of the classroom, the campus and the district. Many teachers know how to reach out to the local community to get help with specific and general needs in the classroom where support and resources are limited.

Understanding and utilizing the *political frame* is not an either/or type of process. It is working with the limited resources available and making it work for students. Sometimes who you know does make a difference, and other times what you know makes an even bigger impact on student achievement. This is especially true when you take what you know and apply it to this *political frame*.

Our fiscal support for public education has been historically very limited with not much additional financial help in the near future either at the local and state levels, but many of you have learned the power of the *political frame* by simply seeking out and identifying the many resources out there that are free and waiting to be utilized. There are dozens of secure viable internet sites that offer a number of additional instructional help aides that give support for improving student academic success. Limited resources and supplies cannot be an excuse for our goal of continuing to improve student achievement. Become adept and knowledgeable of the opportunities the *political frame* has to offer and use them to support improved student achievement. If you do so, your level of expertise and skill as a teacher will improve and so will your students' academic achievement -- and that is why we do what we do.

Leadership Application

LEADERSHIP TOOL: *To develop this leadership tool you will need to understand and utilize the political frame of cognition. Acquiring this tool and using it to its fullest will allow you to utilize the limited resources that are available for public education.* This is an uncomfortable tool to develop for most people because they do not like competing for resources that should be made available for everyone, and it is difficult for educators to get past the realization that this aspect of educating students is unfair. Nevertheless, you should work through your mental processes of accepting this as reality knowing that the situation is unfair and think about doing what is best for your students. Once you rationalize the need to secure resources for your students, then you can begin working on this leadership tool.

LEADERSHIP REFLECTION: Think about the supplies and resources that you need for your class that you do not possess? Do other teachers on your campus seem to have more supplies and resources? If it is so, and I suspect that it is, why is that the case? Consider your campus as a whole. Does your campus seem to have more or less of the district supplies and resources? Again, why is that so as well? If your classroom or campus appears to be on the short end of those available supplies and resources, how can you level the playing field, and who are the major players in obtaining the resources that you need?

LEADERSHIP APPLICATION: Think about the lesson that you just read. If you are a classroom teacher, make a conscious decision to identify your specific classroom needs (not wants) and just as important, identify who controls those resources and where they can be obtained. The general reason for the lack of resources is the lack of money. However, sometimes it is simply the complacent behavior of not asking. No matter how big or small your learning community may be, those in charge do not know all about you and cannot read your mind. They just may not be aware that you need these resources, and you might be surprised at the response you get just by asking. If there truly is a shortfall of funding, consider any philanthropic organizations and community businesses as a source provider for those resources. There are also online philanthropic organizations that will make small donations just by you asking and matching donors to your request. Make a commit to complete one or more of these suggestions and see what happens. Maybe you will get what you need.

LEADERSHIP RESULTS: This is an important part of growing as an educator and as an instructional leader. Take a moment to enter your thoughts in the journal space (as suggested in the introduction) and take a few minutes to reflect on this week's application. Was the application successful? What were some indicators of success? What were the indicators of failure (this is important)? What can you do differently to improve on this particular leadership tool?

RESPONSE:

_____

_____

_____

_____

_____

LEADERSHIP SKILL SET: Developing your ability to become skillful in the political frame will take some time, but you must be willing to step out and test the waters. Do not be afraid of failing. I can assure you now that you will not get everything you need. I can also assure you that you will get more than you had by simply practicing this leadership skill set. Administrators in central office positions have had years of conditioning that there is not enough money to go around, but when they receive personal stories of genuine needs, they typically rally around that cause and find the money, usually in some discretionary fund, to help you with your need. This is especially true when they realize you have targeted your need for improving student achievement. For those educators who have been recalcitrant in attempting to secure resources using the political frame skillset, they are doubly rewarded when this particular tool pays dividends. Take a risk for your students. Begin utilizing the political frame.

They said to Him, "Caesar's." And He said to them, "Render therefore to Caesar the things that are Caesar's, and to God the things that are God's." Matthew 22:21 NKJV

Lesson 24: Frames of Cognition - The Symbolic Frame

I certainly have not seen this in many years, but when I was in high school attempting to play basketball, we had an organized group of high school girls that would show up at all of our basketball games to cheer us on to victory. They would show up in white shirts and have other coordinated accessories, including white gloves, and would sit as a cheer block. Their job was to inspire the crowd and encourage the players to do their best. Looking back, I realized that I noticed them the most right after a big play had occurred or when we needed extra encouragement during a difficult part of the game. They epitomized in some sense what individuals do when they operate from the *symbolic frame* in an organization.

Public school systems need people, many people, who are willing to operate from the *symbolic frame* and serve as an encourager for those around them. I am not talking about or necessarily speaking from the standpoint of being a cheerleader, but more of an encourager and stimulator to help others to keep the faith and the focus on why we do what we do. Every day brings new challenges and issues to be solved and resolved in our profession. People who operate from the *symbolic frame* understand the importance of this leadership characteristic and its impact on building a culture of success.

Bolman and Deal[25] (1997) clarify this frame by advocating that those who possess the capabilities of the *symbolic frame* are both inspiring and visionary. When you think about it, inspiration without a vision ends up being much ado about nothing. Vision without inspiration is like driving a car without fuel; neither one gets very far.

We need people in education who will exercise their ability to be keepers of the vision and who will serve as encouragers during those times when it seems that nothing is working right, and there does not appear to be a light at the end of the tunnel.

Sometimes, the vision can be translated into a constancy of purpose. Stated differently, we are all here to help every student to achieve academic success. If our vision is displaced with anything other than this, then we will meander through the educational process not ever achieving meaning to our purpose and wondering if we are, in fact, making a difference or helping students achieve what will become some nebulous academic success.

The education system needs you. We need people who will demonstrate leadership and provide meaningful, encouraging support to other teachers and staff. We need people who will put on the colors of success and frame the message in ways that others will keep moving toward our common goal. These are not the best of times in education, but this is a time that is ripe for leaders to step forward and be courageous. We need leaders who will turn the dreams of students into reality and student failures into student successes.

A kind word to a fellow teacher or staff member; a note of thanks to an administrator or even a parent may just be the catalyst that keeps fuel in that person's tank for another day. You might even inspire a student to try one more time in an effort to master a specific skill. Pick up the leadership tool and the characteristics of the *symbolic frame* and become a leader – an encourager for others. You be the difference-maker!

Leadership Application

LEADERSHIP TOOL: *This leadership tool is the symbolic frame. You must be willing to make a personal evaluation of your vision for educating students. If your vision is not in agreement or you do not believe that you can make academic differences in the lives of students, then you need to reassess your vision.* Every well-built house has a firm foundation and such is the case for the teaching/learning process. If your teaching pattern is built on something that is fluctuating based on your day-to-day accomplishments, then please take a moment to seriously consider making a more serious commitment to educating students.

146

LEADERSHIP REFLECTION: Do you have teachers or staff members on your campus who seem to go around and help others in a crisis or are always willing to contribute? Are you that person? Do you have people you like to be around because once you have been with them for a few minutes, you feel rejuvenated and ready to go at it again? Is there anyone on your campus that keeps the vision of student academic achievement in the forefront? Is your campus in need of a banner-carrier?

LEADERSHIP APPLICATION: To work in the symbolic frame, you need to start small or you may get a lot of eyebrows raised wondering if you had one too many espressos that morning! Once you have evaluated your personal vision regarding student achievement and you feel that you are maintaining the proper philosophy, subtly look for ways to individually boost a fellow colleague in his/her classroom. You do not have to stand up in a faculty meeting and espouse the vision, but a kind and simple note of encouragement to another educator regarding why we do what we do and thanking them for being a leader in that area would be a great beginning.

LEADERSHIP RESULTS: This is an important part of growing as an educator and as an instructional leader. Take a moment to enter your thoughts in the journal space (as suggested in the introduction) and take a few minutes to

reflect on this week's application. Was the application successful? What were some indicators of success? What were the indicators of failure (this is important)? What can you do differently to improve on this particular leadership tool?

RESPONSE:

_____

_____

_____

_____

_____

LEADERSHIP SKILL SET: Developing the skillset of being able to utilize the symbolic frame can be equally rewarding for both you and the recipient of your encouragement. It is important to be genuine in your notes of encouragement and accomplishments, as well as staying on point with regard to the vision of your campus and learning community. Do not use this as a tool to try to influence an individual to see your point of view or to persuade them to change their behaviors. That kind of attempt could backfire and leave you with a bad taste in your mouth. By the way, do not miss the opportunity to be vocal in a faculty meeting if your administrator or some other campus leader opens the door for you to respond in this area. Just make sure that your comments are energizing with regard to student achievement.

...that their hearts may be encouraged, being knit
together in love,
and *attaining* to all riches of the full assurance of
understanding,
to the knowledge of the mystery of God, both of the
Father and of Christ.
Colossians 2:2 NKJV

Lesson 25: Leaving a Learning Legacy (Giving the Gift of Learning)

As I am writing this leadership lesson, we are nearing the Christmas holiday season, and I am reminded of Helen Keller's life and how she has been an inspiration to me. She made such an impact that I visited the place where she grew up in Tuscumbia, Alabama, so I could envision all the places she walked. While doing this I became more aware of the importance of communication and its connection with learning. However, the story behind the story was Anne Sullivan, her teacher who realized the potential of Keller from the very beginning. It was Sullivan's determination and tenacity that provided the breakthrough of *how* Helen Keller would learn. It was Sullivan's conviction and continuous attempts at communication, as a twenty-year-old teacher, that would *leave a learning legacy* for Helen Keller.

There are children who come into each one of our classrooms every day who are educationally blind and deaf to learning. It is not that they do not want to learn. It is just that they are frustrated with the how of learning. The opportunity for your learning community to *leave a learning legacy* is more than just helping students to learn information. *Leaving a learning legacy* allows us to observe our students learning through intrinsic motivation while learning information is often times more extrinsically motivated by local, state and national expectations.

Your learning community must continue to build a culture that will *leave a learning legacy* for your students. To help provide the gift of learning, we must understand what lifelong learning looks like. DuFour[26] (2005) credits Roland Barth in giving us some insight as to what this might look like. He shares that students would develop a love of learning for its own sake. Students would develop the ability to ask one's own questions and take responsibility for addressing and pursuing them. We would create in our students the capacity to continuously reflect on oneself as a learner and on the learning process. Instead of teachers setting high standards, students would begin to learn the value of setting one's own high standards of learning and to assess the extent to which one is succeeding in resolving the question that may be posed. Moreover, most certainly in *leaving a learning legacy* is the ability to know and to cultivate and celebrate success.

I suspect that many teachers on your campus and in your learning community practice this very concept of *leaving a learning legacy* – the gift of learning. We have teachers who are not just teaching what we learn but how to learn as well. We must be about moving from a culture of teaching to one of learning. This can be accomplished through your classroom leadership setting the example of teaching students how to learn.

I recently attended a funeral of a teacher friend who passed away during the Thanksgiving holidays. She was a member of a Teacher Leadership Cohort that I had lead. Peggy was a Master Reading teacher and a recognized teacher leader on her campus and in her learning community. Those who attended her funeral realized that even in her death, she taught us about life. Peggy left a *learning legacy* with her students and with her colleagues. Like many other teachers before her, we celebrate her success. When you leave the teaching profession, will you have passed along the *learning legacy* to others?

Leadership Application

LEADERSHIP TOOL: *This leadership tool is the tool of developing lifelong learning in your students. The lifelong learning process that you are giving as a gift (learning legacy) to your students can only be developed over time and through a continuous process of communicating the importance of learning.* It important that you demonstrate through communication and by example that you are a lifelong learner or your students will not accept your gift to them. It will remain unwrapped.

LEADERSHIP REFLECTION: Do you continue to read about the latest information on how to teach or how students learn? Have you read any information on brain research lately and what physiological processes occur in learning? Does your campus engage in professional learning communities that utilize time in sharing best teaching strategies being used to improve instruction? Does your campus leadership encourage and provide funding for professional book studies and professional growth for you and other campus staff?

LEADERSHIP APPLICATION: Have a candid and open conversation with your students using appropriate age-related vocabulary, explaining the importance of the students developing themselves as lifelong learners and help them to understand what that means. Share the research on the number of jobs an individual will hold in his/her lifetime and emphasize the importance of how continuous learning beyond the mandatory education years is vitally important. Use your own learning process as an example of the importance of lifelong learning. Begin to create in the students the benefits of becoming empowered as individual learners in charge of their own learning. If appropriate, include a discussion of intrinsic and extrinsic learning and the powerful transformation in their learning will occur when that switch happens.

LEADERSHIP RESULTS: This is an important part of growing as an educator and as an instructional leader. Take a moment to enter your thoughts in the journal space (as suggested in the introduction) and take a few minutes to reflect on this week's application. Was the application successful? What were some indicators of success? What were the indicators of failure (this is important)? What can you do differently to improve on this particular leadership tool?

RESPONSE:

_____

_____

_____

_____

_____

LEADERSHIP SKILL SET: You are leaving a learning legacy. It is your gift to each student. This is promoted and developed over time. It is done with combining other skill sets such as building relationships and providing time on a regular basis to have these conversations. Most students cannot or have not made the connection of why they are engaged in any learning process and how it will apply to them beyond their formal years of education. Once you have communicated on a regular basis the importance of obtaining not just information but also the love of learning then you will have begun to instill a legacy of learning in your students. If even one student notices this process, you will have left a legacy of your own. Then, you will have made a difference in the life of a student!

A wise *man* will hear and increase learning,
And a man of understanding will attain wise counsel.
Proverbs 1:5 NKJV

Lesson 26: Meaningful Work

For me, it was my fifth grade teacher. She was the most significant teacher in my entire life. It was not because she was the smartest, the most creative or even the most interesting teacher I had. In fact, at the time, I did not have fond feelings or even much admiration for her. I detested Thursday afternoons in her class because right after lunch she would begin filling the chalkboard with social study facts about each of the states we were studying at the time. She would start at one end of the board and begin writing and moving down each section of the chalkboard until it was full. Then, she would move to the next section of the chalkboard. When she got to the very end of the chalkboard, she would start back at the beginning, erasing the first section and filling it up with new information. My classmates and I would write the entire afternoon, and if we were not finished at the end of the day, we stayed until we finished. Tests were always Monday afternoons, and we would receive our graded papers back on Wednesday. Though this was only one example of my fifth grade self-contained teacher's instructive ways, what she taught me was what it meant to be a teacher, a student and the *meaningful work* that was created by the process.

This *meaningful work* that I refer to is not a set of standards and outcomes that teachers and students must teach and learn. Yet, *meaningful work* is the teaching/learning process by which there is created a special moment between the teacher and student(s) when knowledge combusts into life-changing learning experiences. *Meaningful work* can transform an individual from being *passive*—a vessel to be filled—to being *active*—a conduit to change one's self and others.

A learning culture that focuses on student success must focus on *meaningful work*. A culture of success understands the objectives are simply the vehicle by which we as educators use as catalysts for the learning. The focus of the organization is reaching students to create this *meaningful work* that will change lives forever. This is the beginning of a lasting culture of success for the classroom and campus as well as ingraining the teaching/learning process for students.

Here is the crucial conversation that we must have among ourselves and in our professional learning communities if we are to continue to build a culture of success within our learning communities. Are we willing to continue to focus student academic success and do whatever it takes, regardless of the influencing decisions that are outside our classrooms that may be beyond our control? Over the 37 plus years of my life as a professional educator, I have spent time in many of the school buildings watching *meaningful work* occur, and my perception is that teachers are still very much creating an atmosphere for *meaningful work* for our students, taking advantage of every opportunity to change lives for the better. I continue to be impressed and blessed by the professional attitudes of educators and our and supporting staff. You are making a difference in the lives of your students.

It was my fifth grade teacher who did that for me. Up until then, school was something I had to do. She taught me the fundamental importance of the learning process, as well as the powerful secret of the potential of knowledge and what it could do for me as an individual and in helping those around me. She helped create a thirst in me to become a better person through the world of knowledge and *meaningful work* as I am sure many of you do for your students.

Leadership Application

LEADERSHIP TOOL: *This leadership tool is about teaching your students the meaning of meaningful work. It is about ingraining the concept of the importance of learning and how this process can be useful throughout the student's life.* You are the teacher and passing this gift along to your students is imperative for them to be successful beyond the days of their required education. Developing this leadership tool within yourself and passing it along to your students helps to provide the fuel for the learning process for your class and for your students' classes in the years that follow.

LEADERSHIP REFLECTION: Do you ever talk to your students about the learning process and the reasons for learning what they learn? Do you take the time to invest in the mechanics of learning? Do you find that you and your colleagues are so inundated with the critical learning mass that you feel overwhelmed with just trying to teach the material that you just do not feel like you have the time to stop and talk about the learning process?

LEADERSHIP APPLICATION: Talk to your students about the learning process and why you believe it is meaningful work. So many of our students do not have a concept of why they are learning the material and the importance of becoming a lifelong learner with an intrinsic process for learning. Talk to them about the different ways to learn material. You can search the internet for "learning strategies" and "study habits" to get some great ideas for students to pick up. Listen to the responses that you get from your students, especially the ones that are reluctant and recalcitrant learners. Make a note to focus on those at a later date.

LEADERSHIP RESULTS: This is an important part of growing as an educator and as an instructional leader. Take a moment to enter your thoughts in the journal space (as

suggested in the introduction) and take a few minutes to reflect on this week's application. Was the application successful? What were some indicators of success? What were the indicators of failure (this is important)? What can you do differently to improve on this particular leadership tool?

RESPONSE:

_____

_____

_____

_____

_____

LEADERSHIP SKILL SET: The skillset that you are developing here to build a cadre of students who understands the impact of meaningful work. You are helping them to transfer the learning process from an external "must do" frame, to the internal side of "self-improvement and gratification" frame. This is significant because it begins to touch the students within rather than superfluously regarding learning, and once they have imbedded the meaningful work process on their side of the brain, then you have created a more successful student and a lifelong learner.

> **And whatever you do, do it heartily,**
> **as to the Lord and not to men.**
> **Colossians 3:23 NKJV**

Lesson 27: Necessary and Noble Cause

I grew up in a time when teachers were revered because of the profession they were in as educators. I can remember walking into my classrooms at a young age, and I would be in awe of the magic and mystique created by my teachers. This was a place of learning, a place where incredible things happened and a place where lives would be touched forever. I grew up in a time where one was taught that his or her only limitation to success in the world was the amount of sweat equity he or she was willing to put into the learning and studies in the classroom. It was a time when teachers relied on parents to help support the learning process at home. It was a time when education was thought of as a *necessary and noble cause.*

What is our *necessary and noble cause*? It is the overarching belief and understanding that what we do as educators in the classroom maintains the civility and stability of our society, perpetuates the common ideals of our nation and stimulates the thinking that causes the creativity for improving our standard of living. This is the *necessary* aspect of our belief. It is a *noble cause* in that educators are the fulcrum by which the ideals and beliefs of our nation teeter. It is refusing to allow complacency in the classroom to become the norm even when the individual learner is willing to accept these changes as inevitable. Our *noble cause* is a higher aspiration than any one of us or even the totality of us all. Our *noble cause* has and will continue to be challenged by the erosion of societal norms, the family structure and budgetary restraints.

The "Leave it to Beaver" student left the classroom years ago and was replaced with students affected by the societal influences, shifting cultural norms, perceptions, and changes fifty years in the making. This, in turn, has resulted in a more challenging classroom for today's educators. Our students need our leadership and courage even more now than they did in previous generations.

Fifty years ago, a student could walk away from formal education and still have some hope of making a successful living. Not in today's technologically and service oriented economic market. It takes brainpower and the understanding of what true lifelong learning means. That is accomplished in *meaningful* learning and also in learning how to learn. If we continue to sublimely write off students because they have chosen not to learn and refuse to hold them responsible for learning, then we start the clock of our own economic and societal demise and that of our educational system; we will be exactly one generation removed from a failed and dismantled nation.

The classrooms across our country are filled with teachers who possess the same core belief that what we do constitutes a *necessary and noble cause*. They understand that we must be about the education of our students so that students can realize the dream of success in a democratic society and a free people. However, we are at an educational crossroads that cries for courageous decisions on our part as educators. As a society, we can no longer afford to allow students to choose not to learn. Our generation cries for a body of educators whose culture is dedicated to achieving academic success for every student – a *necessary and noble cause*.

Leadership Application

LEADERSHIP TOOL: *This leadership tool is a more personal philosophical tool that should be engrained in every teacher. This concept of a necessary and noble cause should be a belief that all educators should embrace. It is a fulcrum of our educational system and our society.* The necessary aspect is that we as educators must never give up on the expectations of student learning, even when the student gives up on himself/herself. The noble aspect of this leadership tool is that we are supporting and adding to our democratic and cultural beliefs that this is the greatest nation on the face of the earth where people have more freedoms than any other nation. To keep it great, we need to build a society of educated people who are stimulated by creative thinking.

LEADERSHIP REFLECTION: Do you ever have thoughts of giving up on individual students as learners and just throwing in the proverbial towel? Do any of your colleagues openly comment that they have given up on a particular student or in a sense, released that student from the responsibility of learning? Here is a question to consider. Does your campus have a high rate of academic failures and is your staff proud or indifferent of that fact?

LEADERSHIP APPLICATION: This is not something that you may outwardly do with students, but this is more of a personal commitment that you must consider as you weigh your responsibility to the adding of competent and productive members (students) to our society. It starts at a young age, and your impact as the students' teacher will last for their lifetime. Will you commit to holding all students accountable for learning and helping to contribute students who will be responsible productive citizens? What will you do differently to demonstrate your commitment to this necessary and noble cause? If you want to include your students, you could ask them to sign a "learning pledge" document that states they agree to the principles of learning and its rewards. But remember, it is your concept of a necessary and noble cause that will serve as the catalyst for student learning. That will take a firm and determined commitment on your part.

LEADERSHIP RESULTS: This is an important part of growing as an educator and as an instructional leader. Take a moment to enter your thoughts in the journal space (as suggested in the introduction) and take a few minutes to reflect on this week's application. Was the application successful? What were some indicators of success? What were the indicators of failure (this is important)? What can you do differently to improve on this particular leadership tool?

RESPONSE:

_____

_____

_____

_____

_____

LEADERSHIP SKILL SET: The skillset of building a mindset that embraces a necessary and noble cause starts with a commitment, a pledge. Sometimes, writing your thoughts down and putting them on paper in a document that you can see helps to bring structure to your thoughts, and it also serves as a reminder of why you do what you do. It is your own constitution for learning and what you will add to the sum of the total of our society. If you are working in a group, this could be a professional learning community project, and you could hold each other accountable. Because after all, what you do certainly is a necessary and noble cause.

Finally, brethren, whatever things are true, whatever things *are* noble,
whatever things *are* just, whatever things *are* pure,
whatever things *are* lovely, whatever things *are* of good report,
if *there is* any virtue and if *there is*
anything praiseworthy—meditate on these things.
Philippians 4:8 NKJV

Lesson 28: Ordinary to Extraordinary – Instructional Strategies that Work: Part I

Have you ever marveled at the number of diet programs that hit the market every year, each professing the one that works? There must be hundreds of diet programs out there. I am always amazed at the guaranteed results that each of the programs provide. The truth is, probably every one of them could help if they were followed with some degree of fidelity by the person trying to lose weight, but I suspect that there are some that are much more successful than others are because they follow some simple truths about weight loss. The same principles of truth apply to the plethora of instructional strategies that are available to teachers in the classroom, and the same principles of fidelity need to be implemented to achieve academic success. To determine *instructional strategies that work*, one simply needs to refer to the data, practice and research that are readily available to educators.

Here are some basic but proven meta-cognitive *instructional strategies that work* if implemented with non-negotiable standards by classroom teachers. We must teach the critical attributes of the curriculum that are closely aligned with the standards for assessment (teach what is being tested). We must focus on instruction, and we must require students to master the instruction (teaching *and* learning). When asked about how he could have failed a grade in school, Winston Churchill was attributed to saying, "I did not fail; I was given a second chance to succeed." He was given several opportunities to learn and to master the required material. To move from *ordinary to extraordinary*, we must move our focus off the emphasis of the grading process to an emphasis on the student mastering the learning standards as established by your local learning community and your state education agency.

You are not going to be blown away by these instructional strategies, but you should be reminded of their extraordinary academic benefits. The first of two important aspects of moving from *ordinary to extraordinary* is to read. We must require students to read...in class...often. Schmoker[27] (2006) quotes a study on reading that concluded, "...the ability to read well is the single best indicator of future economic success, regardless of family background." All teachers must require students to read. This is a proven *instructional strategy that works*.

We must require students to think at higher levels of cognition by asking higher level questions about what they have read and then teach them to think and respond accordingly. This is one of the proven *instructional strategies that work* when moving from *ordinary to extraordinary* in academic success. The students must be given opportunities to think, reflect and respond through the application of the reading process. Reading often builds continuity, consistency, comprehension and competency in the reader. We must attack the critical learning attributes of reading and break those attributes down so we (in every discipline) understand what those critical attributes mean. We cannot teach what we do not understand, and students will not learn what we cannot teach. Reading and learning how to use reading as a tool to advance the learning process is the pivotal component for moving students from dependent learners to independent learners.

The most relevant learning for teachers typically takes place with teachers. This process is called collaborative learning or professional learning communities. All teachers - not just reading teachers – should talk to each other about common assessments, about what worked and what did not work, how strategies were taught, the major critical attributes of the specific discipline, re-teaching strategies and other academically related topics. Notice that all of these topics are instructionally and student focused. Teachers must have time to meet with other teachers of the same discipline to help move the culture of the campus and district from the *ordinary to the extraordinary*.

Leadership Application

LEADERSHIP TOOL: *This leadership tool is that of building your repertoire of instructional strategies that work and recognizing that developing the students' reading skills is crucial to developing students as independent readers and learners. Each teacher, regardless of the discipline that you teach, must have a solid foundation of the critical reading skills that are fundamental for students to move from learning to read to reading to learn.* Using your cadre of professional learning community members is a great starting point for individual teachers to develop a solid foundation of reading skills.

LEADERSHIP REFLECTION: Do you provide time in your classroom for independent reading? Do your students know that whenever they have completed their class assignments that they are expected to pull out a book and read? Do you set high expectations for your students regarding their reading? Does your campus have a set time for independent reading such as DEAR time (Drop Everything and Read) or some other reading emphasis? Does your campus emphasize developing a common set of reading vocabulary words?

LEADERSHIP APPLICATION: Evaluate your personal commitment to reading skills and the amount of time you dedicate to encouraging the development of strong reading skills. If you have not already done so, have a serious conversation with your students about the importance of reading and its function in them becoming lifelong learners. If you feel deficient in understanding the basics of developing fundamental reading skills, solicit the talents of a qualified reading teacher to help sharpen your reading basics. Somewhere in your class time with your students make a concerted effort to emphasize on a regular basis the importance of reading and model those expectations.

LEADERSHIP RESULTS: This is an important part of growing as an educator and as an instructional leader. Take a moment to enter your thoughts in the journal space (as suggested in the introduction) and take a few minutes to reflect on this week's application. Was the application successful? What were some indicators of success? What were the indicators of failure (this is important)? What can you do differently to improve on this particular leadership tool?

RESPONSE:

_____

_____

_____

_____

_____

LEADERSHIP SKILL SET: The skillset you are building here is the emphasis on building reading skills in your students and emphasizing the importance of reading throughout their lives. To do this, you must model reading both inside and outside of the class. Use your professional learning community to develop a repertoire of ideas to promote reading as a learning tool as well as an enjoyable activity. This instructional strategy is an investment in student success.

> **Hear, *my* children, the instruction of a father,**
> **And give attention to know understanding;**
> **[2] For I give you good doctrine:**
> **Do not forsake my law.**
> **Proverbs 4:1-2 NKJV**

Lesson 29: Ordinary to Extraordinary – Instructional Strategies that Work: Part II

I grew up playing basketball in Indiana – a region known as "basketball country", a region where one either played the game or one watched others play it. In fact, I played for the big high school that was depicted in the film *Hoosiers,* so it is easy to understand the rich tradition and culture of success our basketball program enjoyed. Here was the secret to the success of the program. We had coaches (teachers) who focused on the small, fundamental aspects of the game, and the players (students) focused on practicing them until the fundamentals were so wrapped up in the "myelin" effect, the players performed them as second nature. We learned to master the basic principles of the discipline. That simple, yet important fact moved the program from *ordinary to extraordinary.* There was an expectation in which everyone believed and acted in a way that successful results would follow. Each year, there was a move by coaches and players from *ordinary to extraordinary.*

I have read enough books on improving instruction, instructional strategies, leadership principles, goal setting and techniques for reaching those goals to know that there is no magic bullet, no magic wand and certainly no magic canned program that will insure student success.

There are, in fact, some research driven data that do point us to the hard truth about improving student achievement in the classroom and how we can create a culture of success that moves from the *ordinary to the extraordinary*. Real, sustainable academic improvement can only be achieved from within the learning organization - whether it is the learning community, the campus or the classroom. Yes, one single teacher can change the culture of his/her classroom and even the campus by utilizing research-based instructional strategies that work. This process cannot be successfully completed without the wholehearted attention toward the details of two of the most important skills in achieving student success. The first skill was identified in Part I of this article as reading.

The second academic skill that students must master to become academically successful is writing. Writing must become a common expectation in the classroom in all disciplines. Teaching students to write expository, persuasive and analysis papers would reinforce deep learning and critical thinking among students. The National Commission on Writing[28] (April, 2003) stated, "American education will never realize its potential as an engine of opportunity and economic growth until a writing revolution puts the power of language and communication in their proper place in the classroom. Writing is how students connect the dots in their knowledge." Writing is not a discipline that can be mastered completely outside the classroom, nor by one-draft submissions. Students must be taught through the use of appropriate models of writing through scaffolding and then by using agreed upon writing rubric models; teachers must improve the students' skill of writing and help students achieve at a higher level in that discipline.

Until we take the simplest principles of what we know and turn them into applicable strategies by capable teachers, mediocrity will rule the day in our classrooms. There are as many foolproof strategies for improving student achievement as there are foolproof diet programs discussed in the previous lesson, and the outcomes are the same. Unless the strategies are implemented with some degree of fidelity and accountability, our outcomes will become mere empty results, and we will experience the same results as the thousands of diets – a temporary spike in student achievement and then a return to mediocrity and a loathsome acceptance that we are either unable or incapable to do better.

Hard work, dedication and perseverance toward a common goal generate desired results and create a foundation for long-term sustainability. Sustainability is not about doing great things; it is about doing small things greatly. Make a difference, tell the stories of student achievement and begin

175

to call it tradition and build your culture of success so that we can move from *ordinary to extraordinary*!

Leadership Application

LEADERSHIP TOOL: *This leadership tool is that of building your repertoire of instructional strategies that work and recognizing that developing the students' writing skills is crucial to developing students as independent learners as well. Each teacher, regardless of the discipline that you teach, must have a solid foundation of the critical writing skills that are necessary for students to articulate their thoughts in the written word.* Using your cadre of professional learning community members is a great starting point for individual teachers to develop a solid foundation of writing skills. You should be modeling writing as well.

LEADERSHIP REFLECTION: Do you provide time in your classroom for students to respond in writing? Do you require them to write using the standard writing skills and techniques rather than accepting today's phone text versions of writing? Does your campus and campus leadership emphasize and value the importance of developing lifelong writing skills in your students? Are you willing to make the effort to improve yourself in this area?

LEADERSHIP APPLICATION: Solicit the help of a teacher on your campus with a strong background in writing and ask his/her help in reviewing good basic writing techniques. If you do that, you will have a friend for life! Then, transfer those writing reminders and skills to classroom expectations for your students. Make sure that your students understand the writing expectations and that those expectations are clearly communicated to them and then hold them accountable. Students will rise to your level of expectation if you provide them with the support and resources they need to do so.

LEADERSHIP RESULTS: This is an important part of growing as an educator and as an instructional leader. Take a moment to enter your thoughts in the journal space (as suggested in the introduction) and take a few minutes to reflect on this week's application. Was the application successful? What were some indicators of success? What were the indicators of failure (this is important)? What can you do differently to improve on this particular leadership tool?

RESPONSE:

_____

_____

_____

_____

_____

LEADERSHIP SKILL SET: The skillset you are building

here is the emphasis on building writing skills in your students and emphasizing the importance of writing throughout their lives. To do this, you must model writing both inside and outside of class. Use your professional learning community to develop a repertoire of ideas to promote writing as a learning tool as well as an enjoyable activity. You will increase your students' opportunities for success well beyond the classroom if you are able to transfer the importance of clear, concise communication.

I will instruct you and teach you in the way you should go;
I will guide you with My eye.
Psalm 32:8 NKJV

Lesson 30: Our True North

As a child, our family used to buy cereal boxes that had all kinds of surprises inside. I remember one time we received this compass, and a group of us pretended to be in the wilderness. Some of the kids in the neighborhood got together and pretended that we were lost and we used that compass to make it back to civilization. Although it was a toy and probably never worked properly, none of us really understood how a compass was supposed to work. We did not know that because of the magnetic field that encompassed the earth, the needle pointed to *our true north* when it was kept still for a moment and that we could use this constant point of reference to guide us home.

Any company or organization that intends to be profitable or successful must have a set of values and beliefs that serve as a focal point for the organization. Without this *true north* or constant reminder of who we are and what we are about, we will be doomed to meander aimlessly in a day-to-day routine that will consume our thoughts, actions and our responses. The result will be a focus on the process instead of the prize.

Our educational compass should consist of a set of core beliefs. Those core beliefs serve as *our true north*. When the day-to-day business and interruptions serve to distract our attention away from our main responsibility, we need only to look at our compass to find our *true north* to regain our sense of direction. People in education understand that distractions to our instructional focus occur constantly, so we must be diligent about glancing at our compass to make sure we are on the right path.

When student academic achievement is kept in the center of our conversations, then our compass -- our core beliefs, *our true north* -- stay more closely aligned, and we rarely venture far off the intended course. Those core beliefs keep us on course, and we arrive to our destination by understanding the processes that help get us there. We remain grounded to our fundamental purpose as educators.

We talk and collaborate with other teachers and staff about how to interpret instructional objectives, the best way to introduce and measure those learning objectives, the learning challenges our students are experiencing, best practices and how to get it all in under the time constraints tied to the local and state assessments. The campus and learning community's core beliefs should also be discussed and serve to remind us all why we are here and why we do what we do. If our current practices take us away from our intended destination, *our true north*, then, we need to reexamine either our practices or our beliefs.

The going gets tough from day one in the classroom and does not subside. White, Crouse, Bafile and Barnes[29]

(2009) encourage an attitude that is committed to high achievement, high support and high expectations to keep everyone on track for the long haul. In the midst of instructional struggles and trials and seemingly endless setbacks, our educational compass serves as a constant reminder of who we are, what we are about and where we are going.

During those distracting times, we must come together on our campuses and in our individual learning communities to remind each other why we do what we do. I am sure your learning community is about student achievement, focused on the inherent value of every child and his/her right to a high quality education. Educators believe all students can learn at their full potential and that our business is to ensure teaching and learning take place for all students. That is *our true north* and what will guide us home!

Leadership Application

LEADERSHIP TOOL: *This leadership tool is that of creating a personal set of values and beliefs about student achievement that you can vigorously and energetically support. Those values and beliefs must adhere to the beliefs of your campus and of your learning community.* This requires discussion among your professional learning community cohort members and dialogue with your campus staff at some designated meeting or meetings. It is something that should be revisited personally and often for those beliefs to be valid.

LEADERSHIP REFLECTION: Do you know why you do what you do? Do you possess a set of core values and beliefs about students and academic learning that promote a healthy culture of learning in your classroom, campus and learning community? Do your colleagues demonstrate the same beliefs in their teaching actions during the day? Do your campus administrators have the same cultural expectations?

LEADERSHIP APPLICATION: Once you have reflected for a moment on your personal beliefs about the core values of student learning, write them down. When you have an opportunity to meet with the other members of your professional learning community, ask them to do the same. Compare your beliefs with theirs. Do they align with what you believe should be a common set of values and beliefs about learning? Are those beliefs strong enough to establish them as your true north beliefs when the days get busy with unrelated activities?

LEADERSHIP RESULTS: This is an important part of growing as an educator and as an instructional leader. Take a moment to enter your thoughts in the journal space (as suggested in the introduction) and take a few minutes to

reflect on this week's application. Was the application successful? What were some indicators of success? What were the indicators of failure (this is important)? What can you do differently to improve on this particular leadership tool?

RESPONSE:

_____

_____

_____

_____

_____

LEADERSHIP SKILL SET: The skillset you are building here is establishing and emphasizing a set of core values and beliefs that focus on learning expectations for all students. Those values and beliefs should encompass and highlight high achievement, high support and high expectations. Each of those three components is crucial for building that set of personal beliefs for you to be able to consistently refer to them and help you use that as your compass and comfortably find your way home when you are lost in classroom, campus and learning community activities. These core values should not be lengthy but should contain enough clarity to help you to remember why you do what you do.

This is the day that the Lord has made; we will rejoice and be glad in it.

Psalm 118:24 NKJV

Lesson 31: Persistence that Produces Progress

Poliomyelitis, more commonly known as Polio, was a predominant fear of parents in the late 1940s and the early 1950s because of the devastating effect it had on the health of children. Jonas Salk saw this as an opportunity to help rid the world of this very dreaded disease, so he devoted his time and effort to find a cure. It did not happen overnight. Salk's eight-year investment in the cure was a perfect example of *persistence that produces progress*. His years of research finally paid off when he discovered the cure in 1955. Shortly thereafter, the entire country and other nations all over the world began to use the vaccine that Salk refused to patent. Today, it is estimated that less than one percent of the world's population is unprotected from the polio virus and that within the next few years polio will be completely eradicated from the face of the earth. Salk's *persistence produced progress* from which the entire world benefitted.

Educators continue to address the viruses of ignorance and undereducated citizens.
These diseases directly affect the entire fabric of the United States and its survival as a democratic and economic power as well as a continuing to maintain a productive society. The cure is *persistence* in the classroom *that produces progress*. We can immunize our students, one student at a time, with a

focus and dedication that says, "I will never give up on a student and allow ignorance to rule the day."

How can *persistence that produces progress* overcome the societal disease of educational ignorance? It is a cultural thing. An attitude of *persistence that produces progress* realizes that educators know and understand the students and the individual learning challenges that are connected with each of them. It is realizing that this disease manifests itself in thousands of different ways in our students and that we are part of a learning culture that refuses to accept failure as final. It is a culture where educators *persist* until *progress* is achieved.

Pfeffer and Sutton[30] (2000) laid a firm foundation for experiencing success through *persistence that produces progress* when they stated, "There is no learning without error." You can imagine the frustration Jonas Salk experienced by his many failures and setbacks before he realized success. Classroom teachers throughout the country face seemingly countless obstacles to achieving success with each student. We must first accept that where there is *persistence*, there will be repeated failure. Where there is *persistence,* there will also be *progress*. When we do not allow this failure to be final, especially in the life of a student, the student begins to take the necessary risks to *produce progress*.

186

Our learning organization must continue to resolve that student achievement comes first in our culture of learning and that we will demonstrate no less *persistence* in our actions than we want in our students. We will continue to accept the many educational challenges that are presented before us, and we will continue to seek and search for solutions to overcome those challenges. The result will be victory over ignorance, one student at a time, and the eradication of an uneducated people. That victory can be achieved by every individual educator who understands that *persistence produces progress*. Do not give up!

Leadership Application

LEADERSHIP TOOL: *This leadership tool is developing a dogged persistence to ensure every student achieves academic success. You are creating a safe haven for students to understand it is okay to fail as long as they keep trying to succeed.* This is a hard principle for many educators to accept because of their own journey through the educational system. Your persistence for making sure students master educational success will pay off in their success.

LEADERSHIP REFLECTION: Do you have that type of persistence that allows students to continue to attempt to master the critical objectives? Do you have a set of personal expectations that promote a belief in your students that you will expect them to do it repeatedly if they do not meet your standard of mastery? Do you persistently demand that your students learn the material? Do your fellow teachers expect the same?

LEADERSHIP APPLICATION: Many of your students have developed a one-and-done mentality. They think that they get only one shot, and if they fail, they cannot succeed. Many educators also promote this as well. Make sure you are creating a classroom culture that expects the right results rather than just a submission of paperwork. Many students are just slipping by because we are not expecting more from them. Require better results and persist in your expectations for a higher quality of performance. Communicate that perspective in an ongoing dialogue with them.

LEADERSHIP RESULTS: This is an important part of growing as an educator and as an instructional leader. Take a moment to enter your thoughts in the journal space (as suggested in the introduction) and take a few minutes to reflect on this week's application. Was the application successful? What were some indicators of success? What were the indicators of failure (this is important)? What can you do differently to improve on this particular leadership tool?

RESPONSE:

_____

_____

_____

_____

_____

LEADERSHIP SKILL SET: You are building a skillset of persistence with your students' performance at a high level. Persistence like that will require students to redo their work because it was not at your standard the first time. Be prepared for some puzzled looks from your students and maybe even some other staff members. Exceptional results take persistence and time. This is something that students from all spectrums of the learning continuum can benefit. Your results will not be without struggles and additional effort, but the payoff is raised student performance.

I say to you, though he will not rise and give to him because he is his friend, yet because of his persistence he will rise and give him as many as he needs.
Luke 11:8 NKJV

Lesson 32: Prelude to Success

One of my favorite sporting events is the college basketball playoffs. It is the time of year when all of the practice and regular season comes to a head with more than 64 teams being selected for the NCAA tournament. All of the regular season wins are placed aside for the winner-takes-all championship playoff to determine the best basketball team in the country. It is an achievement just to make it to the tournament, and it is an even greater achievement to make it to the "Sweet Sixteen", the "Elite Eight", and the "Final Four". Just to get to the "Big Dance", the teams must have some *prelude to success*. However, to win it all takes planning and hard work from day one.

The same is true for our students who achieve mastery on their "Big Dance" with the local and state assessments that each learning community and state mandates. There must be a *prelude to success* for our students to be successful especially on state assessments. This preparation comes in a multitude of strategies and techniques that are both learning community-wide and individualized by each teacher. They are as important as focusing on a local curriculum that identifies the readiness and supporting standards assessed to teaching testing techniques at an individual level. It is investing in countless hours of extra tutoring of students, researching and implementing the best instructional strategies, re-teaching information, volunteering for Saturday instructional boot camps and working with individual students before and after class. It is all this and more.

Students do not just learn by osmosis. *Prelude to success* is a process of teacher sweat equity that could never be purchased by any amount of money that state or local agencies could afford. *Prelude to success* begins in the heart of every teacher who truly teaches for the right reasons. Deep within those teachers is the idea of working in a culture that wants to make a difference at the individual student level. It is an understanding that failure along the way is only the *prelude to success*. A significantly higher number of teams that win the tournament typically have one or more setbacks prior to winning it all at the "Big Dance".

There continues to be overt signs that education is under the scrutiny of public sentiment, and for education systems to remain a valuable and viable vehicle for instructing students, we must include in that *prelude to success* a major shift on how we do business. Nevertheless, as Dennis Shirley was cited by Andy Hargreaves[31] (2009), the first step in any meaningful change effort is to ensure that each part of the system is supporting the ultimate goal of the enterprise which is student learning. A campus culture that supports student learning has in its *prelude to success* the integral pieces of success for each student. It is teachers with an understanding that every child is different and every day is different, but our focus never changes. We do whatever it takes to reach each student for academic success.

I could fill up many volumes of the life-investments that teachers have devoted toward our students and their mastery of learning. From Pre-kindergarten teachers' meticulous efforts to help children master the ambiguity of the alphabet and our elementary teachers helping students master reading comprehension, to our secondary teachers opening their classrooms in the early morning and after school for additional help in all subject areas, you create a *prelude to success* that translates into individual student learning and a culture of success.

Leadership Application

LEADERSHIP TOOL: *This leadership tool is always creating the mindset of the prelude to success. This prelude can be translated to preparation (on the part of the teacher and student) and practice.* It is coupling the preparation and practice with multiple learning strategies and learning styles adjusted to the specific needs of the student. As we all know, one size does not fit all. It is also being keenly aware that the teaching/learning process is closely aligned to the local and state assessments.

LEADERSHIP REFLECTION: Do your lessons coincide with what the students will be assessed over in your classroom, learning community and state? Are you familiar enough with your assessed curriculum that you can teach them in a way that your students can comprehend and master? Are you using a variety of teaching strategies that touch the learning modalities of your students? Are your fellow teachers on board with teaching the identified curriculum?

LEADERSHIP APPLICATION: Do a lesson review or two of previous lessons you have taught to determine if they are closely aligned with information the students are to master. If you are using a learning community adopted curriculum, are you following that closely, and are you offering ideas and suggestions for improving the delivery of that curriculum? Is your campus on board with making sure the critical attributes of the curriculum are being taught?

LEADERSHIP RESULTS: This is an important part of growing as an educator and as an instructional leader. Take a moment to enter your thoughts in the journal space (as suggested in the introduction) and take a few minutes to reflect on this week's application. Was the application successful? What were some indicators of success? What were the indicators of failure (this is important)? What can

you do differently to improve on this particular leadership tool?

RESPONSE:

_____

_____

_____

_____

_____

LEADERSHIP SKILL SET: You are building a skillset that is the mindset of prelude to success. To do this, it is important to analyze your lessons to ensure they meet or exceed the alignment to what students will be assessed over at the local and state level. Teachers can recapture a considerable amount of instructional time by focusing more on those critical objectives that take a major portion of any state assessment. Give your students the grace to learn the material and by making sure it is the right material. That is the first step to creating a prelude to success! Stay the course.

The plans of the diligent *lead* surely to plenty,
But *those of* everyone *who is* hasty, surely to poverty.
Proverbs 21:5 NKJV

Lesson 33: Remove the Limits

I was driving home the other day and realized that I was in the middle of some road construction repair work that was being completed. The construction crew had placed some traffic cones to strategically limit the traffic flow. Aside from momentarily being constrained by the slower traffic, I began the analogous comparison of the road workers to that of classroom teachers. I realized that the road construction crew was not ultimately trying to restrict traffic flow. They were working on a part of the road that was originally causing problems with the flow of traffic, and they were trying to fix the problem so they could *remove the limits* and allow for a safer traffic flow. The construction workers were working expeditiously to *remove the limits*. That is exactly what the classroom teacher does on a daily basis. They are **instruction workers** trying to *remove the limits* with individual students and the challenges of learning, so they can have a more successful travel on the academic road to success.

Every learning organization emanates a culture, a practice of internalized beliefs and behaviors. Two people who spend time together develop an informal culture. It is human nature. What are the factors that influence the culture of each campus and the learning community that serve the students on those campuses? It is the teacher behaviors and attitudes that we have regarding student learning and expectations for student academic success. The teacher attitudes and behaviors influence the classroom, the perception of the academic discipline, the campus and that culture becomes integrated and reflective in the learning community.

Our culture should reflect an ***instruction worker*** mentality. Like the road construction workers, our ***instruction workers*** (teachers) attempt to identify the learning hazards for each student and then help to repair the perceived hazards or find an alternate route to the same learning destination. Educators find ways to *remove the limits* to student success. We do this in innumerable ways, but one umbrella for *removing the limits* and achieving success is by a process called Response to Intervention. Response to Intervention, or RtI, is a way for educators to come together to collaborate on solutions to learning roadblocks and provide teachers with options and solutions to help *remove the limits* to learning. It is sometimes a process of hit and miss, success and failure, one-step forward and two steps back at times. It is in fact, a capacity building process for students and for educators. Schlechty[32] (2009) states that, "If the performance of America's schools is to improve, it is essential that the school have the capacity to innovate on a continuous basis and in a disciplined way...Continuous innovation is the lifeblood of learning organizations." Take a risk at *removing the limits* to student success. As an instruction worker, you are looking for instructional solutions.

What business are we in? We are in the business of helping every student to achieve academic success. To that end, we must continue to work at *removing the limits* of our students, stretch beyond the perceived capacity of our individual abilities and realize that student success will come when working together as a team of ***instruction workers***. What does your classroom culture say about you? If you are doing whatever it takes, then it says, ***"Remove the limits!"***

Leadership Application

LEADERSHIP TOOL: *This leadership tool is learning to constantly be mindful of removing the limits for students. You are expected to realize each student's potential and operate as an instruction worker to fix the instructional learning difficulties so that you can remove the limits to the student's learning.* Each student and each learning situation is different. You know that what works with one student may not work with the next. Be diligent to use your cadre of staff and professional learning community members to help remove those learning limits.

LEADERSHIP REFLECTION: Are you spending more time identifying what a student cannot do rather than what he/she can do? Do you catch yourself subliminally checking a student out of the learning process because of his learning disabilities, behavior or attitude about learning? Do your resign yourself to thinking that some students just are not going to make it? Are you hesitant to try new instructional ideas because you just do not think you have the time and you are not sure it will work?

LEADERSHIP APPLICATION: Plan a personal meeting with your Response to Intervention specialist (if you have one) and go over specific concerns that you have about the students from your class who may be seeing the specialists for additional help. Be specific about the limits that your students are experiencing and use your specialist to generate additional ideas to help the students individually in your classroom. I would advise you not to use the "group" meeting to dig deeper into finding ways to help your students. A more one-on-one meeting with the RtI specialists will generate more positive solutions, as well as helping you to establish a better professional relationship with your students' instructional support personnel. If you do not have an RtI specialist, then collaborate with a fellow teacher about a specific student using the same process suggested above.

LEADERSHIP RESULTS: This is an important part of growing as an educator and as an instructional leader. Take a moment to enter your thoughts in the journal space (as suggested in the introduction) and take a few minutes to reflect on this week's application. Was the application successful? What were some indicators of success? What were the indicators of failure (this is important)? What can you do differently to improve on this particular leadership tool?

RESPONSE:

_____

_____

_____

_____

_____

LEADERSHIP SKILL SET: You are working to become better at removing the limits. This is also an evolving a process because you are constantly in flux, trying to find the best solutions for all your students who have limits placed in front of their learning. The more you search for answers, the more you will realize that what did not work for one student did work for another. The instructional road is filled with all sorts of shapes and sizes of learning potholes preventing students from obtaining their full potential for learning. You are that student's instruction worker. Remove the limits!

The fear of the LORD *is* the beginning of knowledge,

But fools despise wisdom and instruction.

Proverbs 1:7 NKJV

Lesson 34: Saving Students Using an Educational Triage

I loved watching the popular *MASH* television series in the '70s and early '80s. This cast of characters was portrayed in an interwoven plot of dark comedy, but whenever the casualties appeared, they immediately focused intently on their patients and evaluated the seriousness of each one to determine whose wounds could be tended to later and whose wounds needed immediate attention. The television series was a fascinating look at how medical *triage* worked. They would use all of the resources they had available, along with their medical expertise to bring this *triage* unit to the front lines to cut down on the time between knowing there was a medical problem and addressing the issue so that more lives could be saved. People who have served in medical *triage* understand how important time is in saving a life.

We create *educational triages* every day on our campuses, and in a sense, we are saving the educational livelihood of our students. We have students that have been inflicted with failure based on classroom, state and national standards. Students at campuses throughout learning communities are academically bleeding out. It is incumbent upon educators to continue to mobilize our expertise and resources to stop this academic bleeding and continue to turn our students' academic fortunes around.

What does our *Educational Triage Unit* (ETU) look like? Every ETU has someone in charge. It is a leadership process. It is not about authority; it is about accepting the responsibility for a student's academic success. This leadership is shared depending on the make-up of the ETU for that particular student. It may be the administrator, the Response to Intervention specialist, the counselor, a teacher or someone else who is knowledgeable about the student's instructional issues. The most important thing to remember is that someone says, "I will be responsible for the academic success of this student." The fact of the matter is that when an ETU is in operation, *educational triage* takes on a life of its own. Everyone takes responsibility through a collaborative process, and when that happens, progress occurs. However, at some point the student's homeroom teacher must step up and make sure that the student is educationally served.

Serving in an *Educational Triage Unit* is especially challenging because the academic wounds are usually internal. That means that when an ETU assembles to help a student, we have to be educational physicians and risk-takers. At one end of the process, we must be focused when identifying the specific academic weakness the student is experiencing to the point we can all discuss it with a high level of understanding. At the other end, we must devise instructional regimens that will help the student achieve success. These instructional regimens are what force us to become risk-takers because as in the medical field, success is sometimes trial and error in finding the solution.

It is also realizing that the instructional risks are research-based and directly focused on improving student achievement – another call for leadership among the ranks. Buckingham[33] (2005) explains that leaders need to be mindful of the onslaught of endless waves of programs and trainings that attempt to seduce employees away from the core, which for educators is implementing a managed curriculum, effective instruction and staying focused on individual student success. We must continue to look for and try new ideas. However, we must never lose sight of our core beliefs, focusing directly on our students and their educational needs.

For us, time is of the essence. When we use all of the expertise of an *Educational Triage Unit* and the educational resources available to us, more of our students will achieve success.

Leadership Application

LEADERSHIP TOOL: *This leadership tool is to understand and conceptualize that you have an educational triage available to you as the classroom teacher. There are* *several people that can be at your disposal to help each of your students who need "lifesaving" measure for them to be successful academically.* It is important to know and be familiar with the people on your campus and in your learning community who can offer the necessary assistance with this educational triage. The campus administrator should be utilized as well in this process.

LEADERSHIP REFLECTION: Do you often feel that you are solely responsible for the academic welfare of your students? Do you consider it too much trouble to talk with the educational staff who work with your students during the day or week? Do you often times feel like you are short on the "medical supplies" that you need to stop the bleeding? When you or someone on your campus identifies a problem with one of your students, is your campus quick to mobilize and respond? Do you have the instructional support of your administrative staff?

LEADERSHIP APPLICATION: Make a list of your potential triage staff for your students. Be open-minded as to who all could be included. Consider all of the teachers that may serve the student during the day including music, art, physical education teachers as well as special education teachers, speech therapists, Response to Intervention specialists, administrators and parents. Develop a plan or a process by which all members of your triage are aware of they will be used in case of an instructional emergency. If you are like me, a written plan helps me to internalize the process even more. Discuss it with all the parties concerned so that when there is an issue you can eliminate any wasted time to implement necessary procedures to address the student's academic issues.

LEADERSHIP RESULTS: This is an important part of growing as an educator and as an instructional leader. Take a moment to enter your thoughts in the journal space (as suggested in the introduction) and take a few minutes to reflect on this week's application. Was the application successful? What were some indicators of success? What were the indicators of failure (this is important)? What can you do differently to improve on this particular leadership tool?

RESPONSE:

_____

_____

_____

_____

_____

LEADERSHIP SKILL SET: You are creating an educational triage of which you are typically the leader. Your knowledge of each person's responsibility is an essential element in the success of this process. Communication by you to everyone, especially the parents is extremely important. Too often, we assume that everyone knows what we know and an academic crisis arises because we did not address the bleeding when it first became apparent. This skillset will become very beneficial and productive if you accept the leadership responsibility for your students and move to implement the process.

When Jesus heard *it*, He said to them,
"Those who are well have no need of a physician,
but those who are sick. I did not come to call *the*
righteous,
but sinners, to repentance."
Mark 2:17 NKJV

Lesson 35: Teaching Through the Tough Times

The amount of academic requirements and accountability that have been placed upon educators has increased over the years. That is not a revelation, but it is worthy of stating considering what educators are facing in the impending future. As a young student, I remember the sense of urgency about a nation's supposedly failing educational system because Russia had launched the first unmanned satellite ahead of the United States, and people began to immediately blame our educational system for not leading in space exploration. Even then, I recall the country blaming the educational system for supposedly not producing the world's best and brightest.

The performance stakes are much higher today with state and national accountability standards used to measure learning community, campus, teacher and student performance. New tests in every state continue to be revised and modified to conform to the standards that our nation has placed on educating our students, and we can expect additional changes looming on the horizon that promise to be even more rigorous and may be designed to also measure college readiness standards on individual students. By all accounts, this system of accountability is not going away.

We are also facing the most difficult economic funding challenges that any educator can remember. The current situation in most states forces teachers to meet academic standards with less personnel and resources. The solution to all of these challenges is *teaching through the tough times*. We must continue to have a laser-like focus on student achievement and *teach through the tough times* while others fight for money and resources to protect the classroom environment. We must continue to commit ourselves to the idea that *teaching through the tough times* means we will keep our vision, a commitment to excellence, for every student. The mettle of educators has always been that we will focus on our students and their best interests.

Schlechty[34] (2002) credits campuses that are "working on the work" are relying on teachers who are leaders and inventors in the classroom. Teachers who are *teaching through the tough times* are finding ways to make it work and are focusing on the work. They are making a difference in spite of the socio-economical, financial and societal challenges we face in our classrooms, our campus and as a learning organization.

Fifty years ago, people were predicting the demise of our country because of the poor performing students who were graduating and moving into the workforce of our country. This same mantra of public opinion has continued throughout the decades; this belief is that our nation has a failed educational system. Look around you. The research is replete with academic success. It does not take a rocket scientist to know that the United States is still the number one super power in the world. Every nation turns to our country for leadership and direction when there is strife in other parts of the world. We continue to be the number one economic power in the world. The data shows the United States still controls the economic future of our global economy. Our country has and continues to produce more patents for creative ideas than any other country in the world. We are an innovative and creative nation.

We will continue to be the best because our teachers will continue to *teach though the tough times*. Teachers are the backbone of our great nation!

Leadership Application

LEADERSHIP TOOL: *This leadership tool is to teach through the tough times. It is so easy for educators to get caught up in the political processes of the educational system, but if we learn to tune out the nonessential information being thrown around and continue to focus on working on the work, then these distractors tend to become less invasive, and you will be able to teach through the tough times.* Do not misconstrue the politics of education with the political frame. Those are two different components. Politics are politicians making decisions about education, and the political frame is you vying for the limited resources. Sometimes, teachers just need to get a tunnel vision on what needs to be done and take care of business.

LEADERSHIP REFLECTION: Do you find yourself constantly worrying about school issues and concerns over which you have little or no control? Do you catch yourself joining in the chatter and conversations of other staff members talking about those same issues? Do you catch yourself using these distractors as reasons for why some of your students are not mastering the material?

LEADERSHIP APPLICATION: Yes, I want you to make another list of all of the current distractors in your learning community that you spend time thinking and talking about with others. Go through the list and determine if there are any issues you have identified that you can personally influence and have any effect on changing for the better. If there are any issues you can personally change, place them separately on a new list. The issues you have no influence or control over, cross them out, crunch up the paper and throw it in the trash. Do not give those issues another thought. For the ones you have left, either decide to take some form of action and do something or do the same with those as well and throw them away!

LEADERSHIP RESULTS: This is an important part of growing as an educator and as an instructional leader. Take a moment to enter your thoughts in the journal space (as suggested in the introduction) and take a few minutes to reflect on this week's application. Was the application successful? What were some indicators of success? What were the indicators of failure (this is important)? What can you do differently to improve on this particular leadership tool?

RESPONSE:

_____

_____

_____

_____

_____

LEADERSHIP SKILL SET: You are developing the skillset of teaching through the tough times. It is an attitude you select so you will not be distracted from the main thing. The main thing is student academic success, and there are many political issues floating around in every learning community that will want to draw your attention from doing your job. Do not allow those distractors to rule the day. At the end of the day or the end of the year if you wish, if your students are successful by whatever means you use to evaluate them, then all these political distractors seem to become trivial in light of your students' academic successes.

Let my teaching drop as the rain, My speech distill as the
dew,
As raindrops on the tender herb, And as showers on the
grass.
Deuteronomy 32:2 NKJV

Lesson 36: Thank a Teacher

If you have never observed the start of a NASCAR (National Association for Stock Car Auto Racing) race in person, you are truly missing an experience of a lifetime. Seriously, the sights and sounds of being with one hundred and sixty thousand of my closest friends, as the cars rev up their engines to begin the race, is indescribable! The television views and audio simply cannot do justice to the forty or more high performance engines going full throttle down the front stretch to start the race. My son and I attended a NASCAR event each year as our yearly father-and-son weekend for many years. We have a great time at the event and spending time together.

At one of the races, as we were walking the pit area, we saw one of the NASCAR cars that had *"Thank a Teacher Today"* on the front hood. I thought this was an odd place to see a message to *thank a teacher* in the middle of this amazing racing venue. However, the more I thought about it, the more it made sense. This car was seen by millions of viewers who watched the race, and for a moment, each viewer received the message to take the time to *thank a teacher* - someone who had made an impact on his/her life. Keep reading....

You might think I was going to say our students, our parents, our business community and our community at large need to take time to *thank a teacher* in education who works countless hours to help students achieve unparalleled academic success. Those types of comments are always very much appreciated, but when I receive a compliment or a note of encouragement from another educator, someone who truly understands the challenges we face and the many obstacles that hinder us from achieving student success with every student, it means so much more. When was the last time you took the time and the opportunity to sincerely *thank a teacher* for what he/she did to make a difference in the life of a student?

A learning community that promotes the culture of uplifting and energizing others (the symbolic frame) can help educators get through the tough times. Educators who take time to *thank a teacher* are people who are energizers. Rath[35](2006) states that energizers are people who always seem to give others a boost and are able to help make a good day a great day.

Energizers have the ability to figure out what gets you going, and they can do it in such a way that is sincere and heartfelt. They edify the people who promote a culture of learning and support those around them. These are people who know how to get others started and they make you want to be around them.

Recently, the staff of an elementary campus I was working with took the time to recognize the efforts of two other campuses. They used the opportunity to recognize the hard work and dedication of other educators and supported their efforts. Their actions to *thank a teacher* proved to be tremendously successful in energizing staff members at the other campuses. What great leadership on the part of the staff and administration at the campus who took the initiative to thank other campuses for a job well done! They recognized the value of a culture that supports others in the organization.

Help to maintain a culture of support. Take the time to *thank a teacher*. Your investment will pay dividends, and most importantly, help our students to succeed. By the way, you will be amazed at how good YOU fell as well!

Leadership Application

LEADERSHIP TOOL: *This leadership tool is learning to be conscious about thanking a teacher. When you, a fellow teacher, go out of your way and take the time to sincerely thank the efforts of another educator, it just makes the note more meaningful.* You understand what the other teachers or staff members may be going through and your words of thanks will serve as a source of encouragement and fuel for them to keep on keeping on.

LEADERSHIP REFLECTION: Have you ever taken the time to write a personal note to another teacher just to let him or her know how much you appreciate him or her? Is there a teacher in your life while you were going through school that needs to hear from you, especially now that you are a teacher? What about writing a note to your campus administrator or the secretary?

LEADERSHIP APPLICATION: Okay this leadership application will take only a little bit of your time but will pay immediate returns by the comments received from the person to whom you wrote. Do you want to be incognito? Great! Do that if prefer. My personal experience is that it means so much more when the receiving person knows who it is. When you have done one, try another! This will make your own day.

LEADERSHIP RESULTS: This is an important part of growing as an educator and as an instructional leader. Take a moment to enter your thoughts in the journal space (as suggested in the introduction) and take a few minutes to reflect on this week's application. Was the application successful? What were some indicators of success? What were the indicators of failure (this is important)? What can you do differently to improve on this particular leadership tool?

RESPONSE:

_____

_____

_____

_____

_____

LEADERSHIP SKILL SET: You are developing the habit of thanking a teacher. You want to get into a routine that creates a habit of writing a note of thanks to other teachers and staff members on a regular basis. People will begin to view you as an encourager and someone who serves as a campus energizer. Want to really reach out? Thank a teacher from another campus – someone you had contacts with in one way or another and can offer a note of sincere thanks. The benefits of developing this skillset will be exponential. This leadership skillset provides fuel for the recipient as well as the sender.

> **...in everything give thanks; for this is**
> **the will of God in Christ Jesus for you.**
> **I Thessalonians 5:18 NKJV**

Lesson 37: Tools of the Trade

I love watching television shows where craftsmen remodel houses or take old dilapidated pieces of machinery and transform them into something that looks and works like new again. It is especially interesting to watch how they envision what something should look like and then begin to work out the plan of how to get there. Take a rundown house for instance. The craftsmen who remodel the houses have so many *tools of the trade* at their disposal to renovate the house as they planned. Some tools are general purpose tools and can be used for a variety of jobs, but some *tools of the trade* are specialized for one specific purpose. The craftsmen have to learn how and when to utilize each of these specific tools, sometimes by trial and error and sometimes by seeking the help of another craftsman who has expertise in that area. The best craftsmen are those who have learned how to recognize and use the right *tools of the trade* for the job that is needed at the time.

Educators are craftsmen as well. Each year we walk into a classroom, and the students become our building and remodeling project. We set out to envision what our class of students should look like in approximately nine months from an academic success standpoint, and we begin the journey using our *tools of the trade*. We attempt to mold and shape the students into successful academic learners who will be ready for the next step of the journey.

Just like a craftsman, our *tools of the trade* continue to expand, and we become better at what we do as we learn how to use our tools more effectively. We have many *tools of the trade* that we can utilize. For one, we have an ever increasing number of instructional tools and strategies that grow as our colleagues and we find success in using them. Giving effective feedback, utilizing appropriate academic vocabulary and implementing best practices are just a few of the hundreds of strategies out there as part of our repertoire of tools.

A well-defined managed curriculum is another excellent *tool of the trade* to help us take our students to where they need to be. Having access to this *tool of the trade* means that we can be more assured that we are teaching on what our students will be assessed later in the year. It gives our education craft a common language when we discuss the curriculum, formative assessments, re-teaching, summative assessments, student engagement and consistent curriculum strands.

What is amazing and somewhat distinct about America is that we have high expectations for meeting the standards, the technical side of teaching, and we have an inherent ingrained right to individual student creativity. The

American education system, with all of our tools of the trade, does not try to mold everyone into the same finished work. Zhao[36] (2009) stated that, "Deeply ingrained in the American culture are the fundamental rights of the individual, respect for and celebration of individual differences." We are a nation founded on individual creativity, and this is what continues and will continue to make our nation number one in the world. Educators who provide leadership by continuing to expand their *tools of the trade* and hold dear the individuality of each student are indeed educational craftsmen.

Leadership Application

LEADERSHIP TOOL: *This leadership tool is creating your sense for the need to always be increasing and expanding your tools of the trade. Educators should constantly be on the lookout for educational tools and strategies that might lend themselves to helping students either individually or as a group.* The professional learning community is a great place to begin learning more about up-to-date- strategies, as well as sharing your new ideas. Belonging to professional organizations and attending workshops throughout the year is a good way to gain knowledge on current teaching practices that work.

LEADERSHIP REFLECTION: Do you look forward to attending workshops with the idea that you can take something away to use in the classroom? Do you belong to a professional organization that provides you with opportunities to learn more about teaching strategies? Do you participate in personal growth such as book studies? Does your campus encourage you to engage in professional growth? Are you reading educational journals that support instructional growth?

LEADERSHIP APPLICATION: Find one new teaching strategy to incorporate in your repertoire of teaching tools to use this week. You can use the internet to search a number of ways to find a new tool for your toolbox, or you can use your professional organizations to direct you to so valuable learning opportunities. You can be specific about the material that you want to teach, and chance are, you will have several suggestions on what strategies can be used.

LEADERSHIP RESULTS: This is an important part of growing as an educator and as an instructional leader. Take a moment to enter your thoughts in the journal space (as suggested in the introduction) and take a few minutes to reflect on this week's application. Was the application successful? What were some indicators of success? What were the indicators of failure (this is important)? What can

you do differently to improve on this particular leadership tool?

RESPONSE:

_____

_____

_____

_____

_____

_LEADERSHIP SKILL SET: You are learning how to be diligent in building your instructional toolbox and make it full of strategies and tools that will help you to help your students. An educational craftsman knows that there are many specialized tools that may only be used once or twice a year, but when they are needed, they are very helpful. Be determined to continue to grow in learning more about learning. To help you in doing this, one of the best activities you can do is to share what you have learned with other teachers and staff members. This will reinforce your commitment to growing as an educational craftsman and others will view you as an educational resource. Oh, and by the way, your students will benefit from your efforts as well as you expanding your tools of the trade.

According to the grace of God which was given to me, as a wise master builder I have laid the foundation,

and another builds on it. But let each one take heed how

he builds on it.

I Corinthians 3:10 NKJV

Lesson 38: The Many Lenses of Education

Most of you have probably never experienced this, but if you have poor eyesight like me, maybe you have. When I was a child in the second grade, more and more examples of the lesson were placed on the chalkboard. I found myself asking if I could move closer to the board to see what the teacher was trying to show us. Long story short, I remember getting my first pair of glasses and being able to see the board from my seat. The vivid memory for me was my walk home that day and looking up at the trees and realizing that there were individual leaves on the trees! Then, I noticed that the grass consisted of blades and not some furry looking carpet of green. I was looking at a whole new world with a different set of *lenses* and that has made all the difference for me. I was not looking at anything different than I had before; I was just looking at it differently now. Wow, what an impact looking out a different set of *lenses* makes!

The observance of our educational community at work is similar to viewing what we do from different sets of *lenses*. There are *many lenses of education* for us, and each one has a particular view of what our education system looks like. The *lenses of education* include, but are not limited to, the views of the following: the students, the paraprofessionals, the classroom teachers, the support teachers, campus administration, central office administration, school board members, parents, community and business people, special interest groups and legislators. All of the perceptions using these *lenses* influence and affect the culture of a learning community, and each group views our education system from a different perspective.

It is important for all of us to realize, understand and accept that success is viewed from each of these *lenses* and to admit that our culture is shaped by the perceptions and expectations that are formed about our learning organization through each group. Here is the good news about how these *lenses* affect and shape our learning culture. Though we each have our *lenses*, we are not looking at anything different; we just see the same thing differently. Everyone who is looking through the *lense* is looking for evidence of student academic success from his/her perspective. It is our responsibility, from whatever set of *lenses* we view our learning organization, to provide the best support we can for the classroom teacher. The teacher is the one who views the process from the closest vantage point, aside from the student. The legislator may see student achievement by a set of state standards, and the teacher may observe minute academic gains on a daily basis that may never reach to the level of measurement on a standardized test. One may see relatively little or no gain in academic progress while the other sees tremendous academic improvement.

The key to overcoming the diversity of seeing the same thing differently is to communicate, communicate, communicate with and among each of the constituents, what the goals and expectations are for student achievement and to include one another through this communication process in student achievement that is not measured by standardized assessments. Blase and Kirby[37] (2000) stress the importance of communicating expectations among constituents by clearly communicating those expectations consistently and repeatedly. It cannot just be a set of published core beliefs posted on some inconspicuous wall. When our vested constituents understand the message of what and why we do what we do, then we all begin to focus on the same thing. That process builds a sense of a culture of success among all the constituents. Our goals and objectives become clearer to everyone, and even though we may see it differently, our differences add to improving the chances of success for all of our students. After all, that is why we do what we do. Enjoy your view and appreciate the many *lenses of education.*

Leadership Application

LEADERSHIP TOOL: *This leadership tool is developing a concept and understanding of the many lenses of education*

that are viewing your classroom, campus and learning
community's success. That assessment of your success is
based on student academic performance and your ability to
understand the perceptions and perspectives of the people
who are viewing your success. To fully comprehend and
benefit from this particular leadership tool, it is important to
step out of your particular situation and try to view your
setting from each of the particular constituents' points of
view. When you are able to that, then you will be more
competent in communicating the bigger picture of student
success to your constituents.

LEADERSHIP REFLECTION: Do you ever express some
personal resentment from a comment from a parent, an
administrator or a community person because you feel they
do not understand your situation in the classroom? Do you
ever hear other teachers and staff members commenting
about someone not on your campus who has made a
statement concerning your campus' performance and you
think the person making the comment is not fully aware of
the situation? Have you ever tried to understand a
constituent's concern from his/her perspective?

LEADERSHIP APPLICATION: Here is a very real
opportunity to help everyone see and understand what is
going on in the classroom and what standards are being set
for your students in your classroom and your campus. Start

by composing a note about your class and the learning expectations for your students. There is much more to be done, but that is a start. Run it by your campus principal to make sure he/she approves of the document. Once approved, disseminate it to your parents. In today's technology, this can be done in a number of ways, and I would suggest that you utilize as many of those venues as possible. Here are some suggestions. You can use the postal service and mail the letter home. Place the note on your school website and make sure your parents are aware it is there. Send the note home with your students in a folder that is to be checked weekly by the parents. Do a video and place the video on your school classroom website. The purpose is to communicate your academic expectations. Do it repeatedly. When you have a parent night, repeat the information to them. It takes many types of communication with repetition to begin to effectively communicate your standards and expectations to your constituents.

LEADERSHIP RESULTS: This is an important part of growing as an educator and as an instructional leader. Take a moment to enter your thoughts in the journal space (as suggested in the introduction) and take a few minutes to reflect on this week's application. Was the application successful? What were some indicators of success? What were the indicators of failure (this is important)? What can

you do differently to improve on this particular leadership tool?

RESPONSE:

_____

_____

_____

_____

_____

LEADERSHIP SKILL SET: Your skillset here is to understand the value of the many lenses of education. Step out of your own set of lenses and attempt to view from each of the perspectives listed in the leadership lesson above and see if you can understand their concerns from that particular set of lenses. Sometimes, it is just a lack of information. Other times, you may see a problem from their lens that was not apparent from your particular perspective. The benefit of this skillset is that you develop a broader perspective of the bigger picture and that turns into useful information and more productive dialogue between you and your constituents.

So Jesus had compassion and touched their eyes. And immediately their eyes received sight, and they followed Him. Matthew 20:34 NKJV

Lesson 39: We Have Them for a Season

I am not a gardener, but I enjoy reading and learning about gardening. I have read on a couple of occasions that it could take ten plus years for an apple tree to produce fruit from a seedling. That means if I grow my own fruit, I have to wait at least ten full seasons to reap the harvest. That is why I shop at the local market for my apples. I am impatient. I want results and I want them today!

An analogy can also be drawn with the students we have in class. We are the educational gardeners, and we have our students *for a season*. Sometimes, it is very difficult for teachers at the younger grade levels to look down the road and picture the mature, fruit-producing student. Just like the apple seedling, it takes ten plus years to bear the fruits of our labor which results in a diploma for the student. That does not mean that we cannot see growth when *we have them for a season*. The truth is we see significant growth in most of our students during the time we have them. Our education system has been designed so we can pinpoint and identify growth over the nine to ten month period of time they are typically in our classrooms.

Here is a major difference between educational gardeners and gardeners of the produce kind. *We have them for a season.* We have little or no control over the educational gardener before us, and we have little or no control over the teacher who will have the student after us. The success of our students bearing the desired outcome from our educational system is clearly dependent upon the numerous teachers that student will have over his/her twelve to thirteen years of formal education.

Since we only *have them for a season*, it is crucial for us to keep our focus on instruction to prepare them for success now, as well as the next level. Educating our students has no dormant season when it comes to learning. And yes, the quality of the teacher is the most significant indicator of student success. Monk[38] (1994) states that the most important variable in student success is what teachers do, not what they know. What you do with students and how they react to your teaching strategies is more important than what you know. Knowledge is only dormant material until you put it into practice for the benefit of your students.

When we put our educational gardening skills to good work and apply the most recent professional development ideas in the classroom, student achievement and growth occur.

I was visiting recently with a first grade teacher, and she was commenting that as she looked upon her classroom in the spring, she marveled at how far the students had progressed since the beginning of the year. She stated that the students could not have performed the instructional activities they were doing now at the beginning of the year. Yet, the day-to-day growth seemed minuscule by comparison.

Your season with your students is now. How will each of us measure ourselves against the continuum of lifelong learning that our students are experiencing and each of our momentary responsibilities to instruct them? When your current students are promoted or assigned to the next educational gardener, will you pass them on with the confidence that they are prepared and ready for continued educational growth on that learning continuum?

When *you have them for a season*, you shape them and influence them for the rest of their lives. Thank you for making a difference.

Leadership Application

LEADERSHIP TOOL: *This leadership tool is learning how to be the educational gardener for your students because you only have them for a season. You will need to become proficient at pruning the unnecessary vines that do not produce the fruit and make sure you provide the necessary educational nutrients and watering for your students to grow while you have them.* Depending on the grade level you teach, you may or may not get to see the fruits of your labor, the awarding of the diploma, but you can know with a high degree of assurance that you played a part in each student's success.

LEADERSHIP REFLECTION: Do you have a clear understanding of your full responsibilities for taking your students from point A to point B? Do you have a mental picture in your mind of what your students need to know and be able to do when they walk out of your classroom at the end of the school year? Do you know what activities and strategies will need to be in place to make sure your students are successful?

LEADERSHIP APPLICATION: Just like a gardener, an educational gardener needs tools to promote educational success for students. What are the tools that you have at your disposal? Are there any other instructional gardening tools that you need that are not available? Familiarize yourself with your curriculum enough to know what, when, where, why and how to use that curriculum to help your students to grow throughout the year.

LEADERSHIP RESULTS: This is an important part of growing as an educator and as an instructional leader. Take a moment to enter your thoughts in the journal space (as suggested in the introduction) and take a few minutes to reflect on this week's application. Was the application successful? What were some indicators of success? What were the indicators of failure (this is important)? What can

you do differently to improve on this particular leadership tool?

RESPONSE:

_____

_____

_____

_____

_____

LEADERSHIP SKILL SET: You are the educational gardener for your students. You just have to get your hands dirty. And, if you are familiar with organic gardening, you know that sometimes it just stinks. That is the same way in the classroom. You are assigned a specific job with specific responsibilities, and there are just some parts of the learning process that are long, laborious and just plain stink. However, if you are going to get from point A to point B, you have to take care of the less glamorous part of teaching. Remember that you just have the students for a season, and the other gardeners are dependent upon you to do your part so that the student bares fruit in season.

To everything *there is* a season,
A time for every purpose under heaven:
A time to be born, And a time to die;
A time to plant, And a time to pluck *what is* planted;

A time to kill, And a time to heal;

A time to break down, And a time to build up;

Ecclesiastes 3:1-3 NKJV

Lesson 40: Finish Strong

I enjoy watching competitions that take longer than a few moments to complete like long distance endurance races and auto racing. Believe it or not, there is a strategy involved in performing well and winning. For long distance runners, it is the knowledge of how to pace oneself and where the runner needs to be positioned to *finish strong*. In auto racing, it is breaking down the race into a series of actions, knowing when to take a pit stop and making the most of those brief stops to help the racer *finish strong*. In both of these analogies, the fastest runner or racer does not necessarily finish first; the winner is usually the one who pays attention to the details along the way, which allows the competitor to *finish strong*. In all cases, the person is required to cross the finish line.

Where is your finish line? We are in the education business, and the culture of our learning communities is that we always take the opportunity to help students learn. It is easy to see that the official start of our academic race or competition is the start of the school year, but there are hours and hours of preparation prior to the start of the big race. Teachers, staff and administrators spend the summer getting ready for their race. Your learning community is committed to helping all students *finish strong* and understands that there are countless decisions and actions that need to take place before the student shows up. The *race* is a long, and sometimes arduous, procedure that helps each individual student *cross the finish line* in the learning process.

To *finish strong* we believe every day is an opportunity to change a student's life.
Deep learning can happen after state assessments have been completed and put to rest. This concept of finishing strong is the idea that our students understand that they achieve success upon the shoulders of their teachers and staff through the observation, analysis, leadership, high expectations, building of relationships, quality teaching, vision, communication, commitment, collaboration, cooperation, determination, support and the willingness of a dedicated staff to *finish strong* for the benefit of each student.

No matter where you serve in your learning organization, each of you has the potential to significantly affect both the students you serve and the culture you create. Author Billy Hopkin[39] (1994) said it best when he said that a leader is one who creates a learning environment with the primary goal of optimal performance and learning by all children. A leader in the classroom establishes a school climate where students can learn through the failures of trying repeatedly. It is through this incubation of learning that the endurance race seems almost too much to manage, but it just may be that a student, or reluctant learner, has the light come on in late May because you chose to *finish strong* knowing that every day is an opportunity for a major learning breakthrough.

I give kudos to the teachers and staff members who recognize how commitment and dedication affect the students in your classrooms each and every day. Teachers who continue to have a lasting impact on the learner and the learning environment are the ones who *finish strong*. When the last student has left your classroom at the end of the year and you have completed all your paperwork, enjoy your summer…and grow!

Leadership Application

LEADERSHIP TOOL: *This leadership tool should be fairly easy to identify, but just to be clear the tool is to finish strong. This is a leadership tool because it is a choice by educators at or toward the end of the school year to make a decision about learning.* I am not talking about or inferring that teachers and students should not take a moment or a day to stop and celebrate that the state assessments are behind them. You should do this in an appropriate manner though. What you need to continue to do as classroom teachers is to refocus your efforts and make all possible use of the instructional time that we have given to you. Finish strong for your students.

LEADERSHIP REFLECTION: If you are an experienced teacher, think back to previous years and consider the amount of instructional time that was underutilized toward the end of the school year. Could you have done a better job of focusing on critical learning objectives after assessments have been administered? Are there teachers and staff members that subliminally consider school is unofficially over when the state assessments have been administered? Are teachers and staff removing learning prompts from the walls and halls long before they should be removed?

LEADERSHIP APPLICATION: Make a mental note not to allow valuable learning and instructional time to be wasted on too many post-assessment activities that do not add to the students' body of knowledge. Review your specific campus instructional goals and objectives and determine if your students have met all of them and what critical objectives could be reinforced to support student success at the next level. Collaborate with your grade level teachers and with your campus administration to help create an atmosphere to finish the instructional year strong.

LEADERSHIP RESULTS: This is an important part of growing as an educator and as an instructional leader. Take a moment to enter your thoughts in the journal space (as suggested in the introduction) and take a few minutes to reflect on this week's application. Was the application successful? What were some indicators of success? What were the indicators of failure (this is important)? What can you do differently to improve on this particular leadership tool?

RESPONSE:

_____

_____

_____

_____

_____

LEADERSHIP SKILL SET: This may be a more challenging skillset to establish if you are working in a school with a climate of subliminally relaxing the instructional focus after the state assessments have been administered. An individual teacher or staff member can easily acquire this skillset, but it will take some commitment and a little tenacity on your part. It is better if you can collaborate with your professional learning community early on to establish some common learning expectations for your students. By the way, this can be done in a fun and exciting way for students if the campus invents some creative ways for students to learn. You never know. You just might surprise yourself and your students!

I press toward the goal for the prize of

the upward call of God in Christ Jesus.

Philippians 3:14 NKJV

Concluding Remarks

You have finished this book, its lessons and applications. Now what? Our education system is filled with teachers and administrators who have the knowledge about what to do. What our education system needs are educators with the leadership courage to apply that knowledge in a meaningful way, to make a difference with the students who are waiting for someone to ignite the fire of learning beneath them.

Education needs people who are willing to be risk-takers and go the extra mile for students. These leadership lessons are a beginning point for the educators serious about change. Change is a constant part of the education process and when that ingredient is mixed with an educator who is committed to the continuous improvement process, the product will be students who are authentically engaged in learning.

If you earnestly apply these leadership lessons on a regular basis, other educators will take notice and want to emulate your actions. That becomes a demonstration in the fractal leadership lesson mentioned in this book. You begin modeling by doing and as others see your positive results, they will want to begin practicing what you are doing, and growth will occur on a wider scale.

You be the difference and enjoy your success!

Endnotes and Bibliography

[1] Stiggins, R. (2003, July). *New beliefs, better assessments.* Presented at the Professional Learning Communities at Work Institute, San Diego, CA.

[2] Coyle, Daniel. (2009). The talent code. New York: A Bantam Dell.

[3] Payne, Ruby K. (2006). *A Framework for Understanding Poverty.* Highlands, TX: Aha! Process, Inc.

[4] Thernstrom, A. and Thernstrom S. (2004). *No Excuses: Closing the Racial Gap in Learning.* New York, NY: Simon & Schuster Paperbacks.

[5] Reeves, Douglas B. (2006). *The Learning Leader: How to Focus School Improvement for Better Results.* Alexandria, VA. Association for Supervision and Curriculum Development.

[6] DuFour, Richard (2004). Whatever it takes: How professional learning communities respond when kids don't learn. Bloomington, IN. National Educational Service.

[7] Tennyson, Sir Alfred Lord, (1833). *Ulysses.*

[8] Pink, Daniel H. (2009). Drive: the surprising truth about what motivates us. New York, NY. Penguin Group.

[9] Bolman, Lee G., Deal, Terrence E. (1997). Reframing organizations: artistry, choice, and leadership. Jossey-Bass. San Francisco, CA.

[10] Tichey, Noel M. (2002). The leadership engine: how winning companies build leadership at every level. New York, NY. HarperCollins Publishers, Inc.

[11] Ibid.

[12] National Society for the Gifted and Talented website: http://www.nsgt.org/articles/index.asp.

[13] Schlechty, Phillip C. (2002). Working on the work. San Francisco, CA. Jossey-Bass.

[14] Lickona, T., & Davidson, M. (2005). Smart and good high schools; Integrating excellence and ethics for success in school, work and beyond. Cortland, New York: Center for the 4th and 5th R's (Respect and Responsibility).

[15] Cotrell, David, Harvey, Eric. (2004). Leadership Courage. The Walk the Talk Company, Dallas, TX.

[16] Wheatley, Margaret J. (1999). Leadership and the new science: discovering order in a chaotic world. San Francisco, CA. Berrett-Koehler Publishers, Inc.

[17] Coyle, Daniel (2009). The talent code. New York: A Bantam Dell.

[18] Ibid.

[19] Hawkins, Billy C. (1994). Educating all students: a pathway to success. Lansing MI, Shinsky Seminars, Inc.

[20] Reeves, Douglas B. (2009). Leading change in your school: how to conquer myths, build commitment, and get results. Alexandria, VA. Association for Supervision and Curriculum Development.

[21] Burns, James MacGregor. (1978). Leadership. Harper & Row, United States.

[22] Bolman, L.G., & Deal, T.E. (1997). Reframing organizations: artistry, choice, and leadership. San Francisco: Jossey-Bass.

[23] Ibid.

[24] Ibid.

[25] Ibid.

[26] DuFour, Richard., Eaker, Robert., DuFour, Rebecca. (2005). On common ground. Bloomington, IN: Solution Tree.

[27] Schmoker, Mike (2006). Results now: how we can achieve unprecedented improvements in teaching and learning. Alexandria, Virginia: ASCD.

[28] National Commission on Writing. (2003, April). The neglected "R": the need for a writing revolution. The College Board.

[29] White, Michael. Crouse, Amy. Bafile, Carea. Barnes, Harry. (2009). Extraordinary teachers: teaching for success. Englewood, CO. The Leadership Learning Center.

[30] Pfeffer, Jeffrey. Sutton Robert I. (2000). The knowing-doing gap: how smart companies turn knowledge into action. Boston, MA: Harvard Business School Press.

[31] Hargreaves, Andy., Fullan, Michael. (2009). Change wars. Bloomington, IN. Solution Tree.

[32] Schlechty, Phillip C. (2009). Leading for learning: how to transform schools into learning organizations. Jossey-Bass. San Francisco, CA.

[33] Buckingham, M. (2005). *The one thing you need to know: About great managing, great leading and sustained individual success.* New York: Free Press.

[34] Schlechty, Phillip C., (2002).Working on the work: an action plan for teachers, principals, and superintendents. San Francisco, CA. Jossey-Bass.

[35] Rath, Tom. (2006). Vital friends: the people you can't afford to live without. New York, New York. Gallup Press.

[36] Zhao, Yong. (2009). Catching up or leading the way: American education in the age of globalization. Alexandria, VA. Association for Supervision and Curriculum Development.

[37] Blase, Joseph. Kirby, Peggy C. (2000). Bringing out the best in teachers: what effective principals do. Thousand Oaks, CA. Corwin Press, INC.

[38] Monk, D. H. (1994). Subject Area preparation of secondary mathematics and science teachers and students achievement. *Economics of Education Review*, 13(2), 113-117.

[39] Hawkins, Billy C. (1994). Educating all students: a pathway to success. Lansing, Michigan, Shinsky Seminars, Inc.

Bibliography

Blase, Joseph. Kirby, Peggy C. (2000). Bringing out the best in teachers: what effective   principals do. Thousand Oaks, CA. Corwin Press, INC.

Bolman, L.G., & Deal, T.E. (1997). Reframing organizations: artistry, choice, and leadership. San Francisco: Jossey-Bass.

Buckingham, M. (2005). *The one thing you need to know: About great managing, great leading and sustained individual success.* New York: Free Press.

Burns, James MacGregor. (1978). Leadership. Harper & Row, United States.

Cotrell, David, Harvey, Eric. (2004). Leadership Courage. The Walk the Talk Company, Dallas, TX.

Coyle, Daniel (2009). The talent code. New York: A Bantam Dell.

DuFour, Richard., Eaker, Robert., DuFour, Rebecca. (2005). On common ground. Bloomington, IN: Solution Tree.

DuFour, Richard (2004). Whatever it takes: How professional learning communities respond when kids don't learn. Bloomington, IN. National Educational Service.

Hargreaves, Andy., Fullan, Michael. (2009). Change wars. Bloomington, IN. Solution Tree.

Hawkins, Billy C. (1994). Educating all students: a pathway to success. Lansing, Michigan, Shinsky Seminars, Inc.

Lickona, T., & Davidson, M. (2005). Smart and good high schools; Integrating excellence and ethics for success in school, work and beyond. Cortland, New York: Center for the 4th and 5th R's (Respect and Responsibility).

Monk, D. H. (1994). Subject Area preparation of secondary mathematics and science teachers and students achievement. *Economics of Education Review*, 13(2), 113-117.

National Commission on Writing. (2003, April). The neglected "R": the need for a writing revolution. The College Board.

National Society for the Gifted and Talented website: http://www.nsgt.org/articles/index.asp.

Payne, Ruby K. (2006). *A Framework for Understanding Poverty*. Highlands, TX: Aha! Process, Inc.

Pfeffer, Jeffrey. Sutton Robert I. (2000). The knowing-doing gap: how smart companies turn knowledge into action. Boston, MA: Harvard Business School Press.

Pink, Daniel H. (2009). Drive: the surprising truth about what motivates us. New York, NY. Penguin Group.

Rath, Tom. (2006). Vital friends: the people you can't afford to live without. New York, New York. Gallup Press.

Reeves, Douglas B. (2009). Leading change in your school: how to conquer myths, build commitment, and get results. Alexandria, VA. Association for Supervision and Curriculum Development.

Reeves, Douglas B. (2006). *The Learning Leader: How to Focus School Improvement for Better Results*. Alexandria, VA. Association for Supervision and Curriculum Development.

Schlechty, Phillip C. (2009). Leading for learning: how to transform schools into learning organizations. Jossey-Bass. San Francisco, CA.

Schlechty, Phillip C., (2002).Working on the work: an action plan for teachers, principals, and superintendents. San Francisco, CA. Jossey-Bass.

Schmoker, Mike (2006). Results now: how we can achieve unprecedented improvements in teaching and learning. Alexandria, Virginia: ASCD.

Stiggins, R. (2003, July). *New beliefs, better assessments.* Presented at the Professional Learning Communities at Work Institute, San Diego, CA.

Tennyson, Sir Alfred Lord, (1833). *Ulysses.*

Thernstrom, A. and Thernstrom S. (2004). *No Excuses: Closing the Racial Gap in Learning.* New York, NY: Simon & Schuster Paperbacks.

Tichey, Noel M. (2002). The leadership engine: how winning companies build leadership at every level. New York, NY. HarperCollins Publishers, Inc.

Wheatley, Margaret J. (1999). Leadership and the new science: discovering order in a chaotic world. San Francisco, CA. Berrett-Koehler Publishers, Inc.

White, Michael. Crouse, Amy. Bafile, Carea. Barnes, Harry. (2009). Extraordinary teachers: teaching for success. Englewood, CO. The Leadership Learning Center.

Zhao, Yong. (2009). Catching up or leading the way: American education in the age of globalization. Alexandria, VA. Association for Supervision and Curriculum Development.

Made in the USA
Coppell, TX
23 September 2021